THE HISTORY OF
RELIGION

To Philip, Gillian, Kate, Emma,
Mattie and Kezia

This edition published by Barnes &
Noble, Inc., by arrangement with
Octopus Publishing Group Limited

2001 Barnes and Noble Books

First published in the UK 1998 as
Hamlyn History of Religion by Hamlyn,
a division of Octopus Publishing Group
Limited

ISBN 0-7607-2695-7

M 10 9 8 7 6 5 4

Printed and bound in China

THE HISTORY OF
RELIGION

KAREN FARRINGTON

BARNES
&NOBLE
BOOKS
NEW YORK

CONTENTS

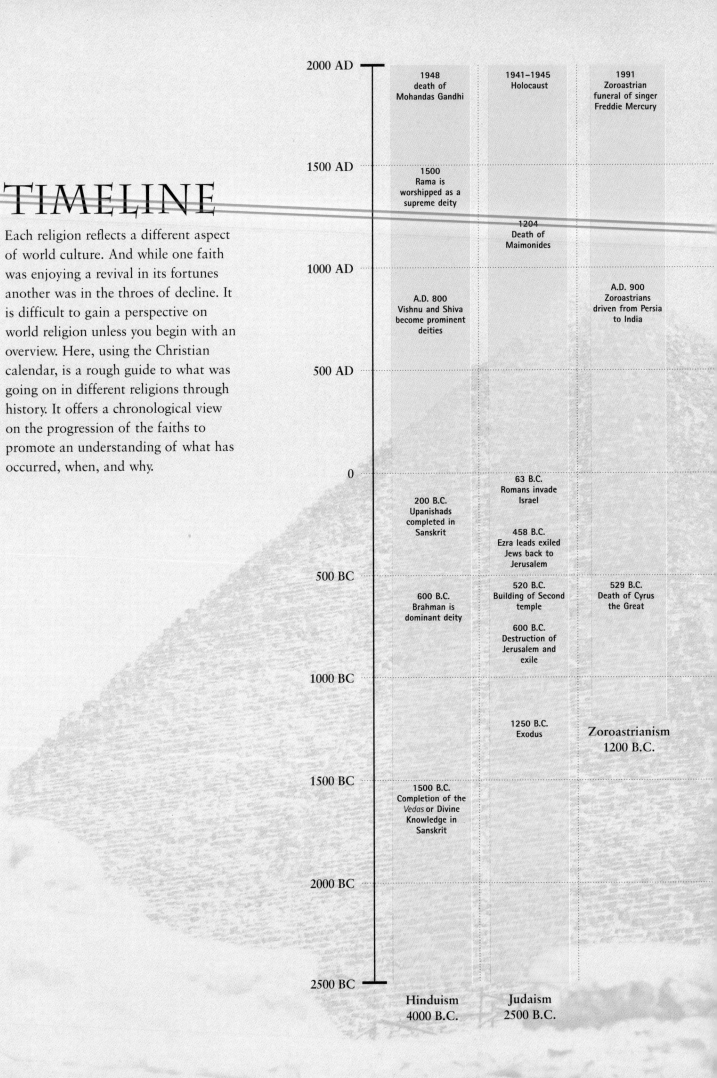

TIMELINE

Each religion reflects a different aspect of world culture. And while one faith was enjoying a revival in its fortunes another was in the throes of decline. It is difficult to gain a perspective on world religion unless you begin with an overview. Here, using the Christian calendar, is a rough guide to what was going on in different religions through history. It offers a chronological view on the progression of the faiths to promote an understanding of what has occurred, when, and why.

	Hinduism	Judaism	
2000 AD	1948 death of Mohandas Gandhi	1941–1945 Holocaust	1991 Zoroastrian funeral of singer Freddie Mercury
1500 AD	1500 Rama is worshipped as a supreme deity	1204 Death of Maimonides	
1000 AD	A.D. 800 Vishnu and Shiva become prominent deities		A.D. 900 Zoroastrians driven from Persia to India
500 AD			
0	200 B.C. Upanishads completed in Sanskrit	63 B.C. Romans invade Israel	
		458 B.C. Ezra leads exiled Jews back to Jerusalem	
500 BC	600 B.C. Brahman is dominant deity	520 B.C. Building of Second temple	529 B.C. Death of Cyrus the Great
		600 B.C. Destruction of Jerusalem and exile	
1000 BC			
		1250 B.C. Exodus	Zoroastrianism 1200 B.C.
1500 BC	1500 B.C. Completion of the *Vedas* or Divine Knowledge in Sanskrit		
2000 BC			
2500 BC	Hinduism 4000 B.C.	Judaism 2500 B.C.	

							2000 AD

1966
Cultural Revolution
attempts to destroy
Confucianism

1984
Storming
of the Golden
Temple at Amritsar

1536
Church of England
founded
1517
Lutheranism

1707
The Age of the Book
begins

1500 AD

**Sikhism
A.D. 1500**

1109–1235
Crusades
1100s
Emergence of
monasticism

1300
Creation of Whirling
Dervishes

1054
East-West Schism

1000 AD

A.D. 632
Death of
Muhammad
A.D. 622
Start of Muslim
Calendar

A.D. 637
Birth of Hui-neng
and Zen Buddhism

**Islam
A.D. 622**

A.D. 500
11 Angas fixed

500 AD

A.D. 110
Four gospels
A.D. 30
Death of Jesus

0

**Christianity
A.D. 4**

275 B.C.—Death of
Chuang Tzu

232 B.C.
Death of missionary
king Emperor
Ashoka

479 B.C.
Confucius dies

500 BC

**Buddhism
500 B.C.**

**Confucianism
500 B.C.**

**Jainism
600 B.C.**

**Taoism
600 B.C.**

1000 BC

1500 BC

2000 BC

2500 BC

INTRODUCTION

In his darkest hour it has taken more than food and water to sustain benighted man. Religion has been his comforter, his prop, his reason for existing. This common thread has united the peoples of the globe throughout the ages, from the Neanderthals to the present day.

It doesn't take a philosopher's intellect to work out why faith in a god has played such a vital role. Life is inevitably followed by death, and then, who knows? Man desires to place order amid chaos and perceive with certainty why particular events happen in life and what occurs beyond the barrier of death. So the prospect of a hidden deity imposing his structured will on earth is an appealing one. Man steals back a modicom of control through appeasement of the god or gods via prayers, sacrifices, piety, and charity.

Religion comes naturally to most of us. It has been the inspiration for wonderful music and fabulous works of art. Themes of good and evil, right and wrong, and strength through faith have been the focus of literature. Even in today's largely secular society we are brought up on the stories and fables inherited from our forefathers. It's impossible to anticipate the effect on our outlook in adulthood but it does tell us something about the courage of those who broke away from instituted religions they had known from childhood to begin afresh. Thanks to the brave hearts new religions have been born, evolved, and, in some cases, died leaving us in the 21st century with a fascinating array of beliefs. A surprising number of religions place emphasis on one Creator god although Buddhism does not acknowledge a god at all. This is just one contrast among many. Some demand celibacy while others preach the virtues of procreation. To some gods the sight of a shaven head is apparently pleasing while others bless the uncut hair. The majority bear a message of peace yet religion has been the root cause of vast numbers of wars and atrocities.

Before religion can work, reason and rationality must be suspended. Seemingly preposterous claims of miracles and meetings with God made by the founders of the great religions, including Judaism, Christianity, and Islam, have been vouchsafed as genuine by thousands of millions of people in the past two thousand years or more.

Some people believe that a god launched the moon into orbit or slowed down the passage of the sun to make a day. Their faith, just like their god, is intangible but remains a cornerstone of their very existence. It's a trump card or an afterlife insurance policy.

These days the supernatural element of religion attracts more imponderable questions and increasing amounts of scepticism. But until science can convincingly explain away the Creation of the world and all within it religion will continue its irresistible rise.

CHAPTER ONE

WORSHIP IN THE

ANCIENT WORLD

Man's evolution remains a perplexing subject, despite many educated guesses and happy archeological accidents. Ancient remainders do exist although previous civilizations have inadvertently erased much of the evidence. With no written tradition, even relatively modern cultures, like those of the 14th-century Aztecs, are clouded by mystery.

For the loss of countless primitive traditions, we may blame the colonialists and the missionaries of recent centuries. Convinced of their own worth, they refused to countenance any other beliefs, particularly those held by people of what they thought to be inferior cultures. Unlike the anthropologists who came later, they did not listen to the natives. The few who did pay heed made comparative interpretations with their own religion, frequently Christianity, and the essence of the indigenous faith and the harmony with which primitive man lived with nature was lost. Today attempts are being made to redress the balance.

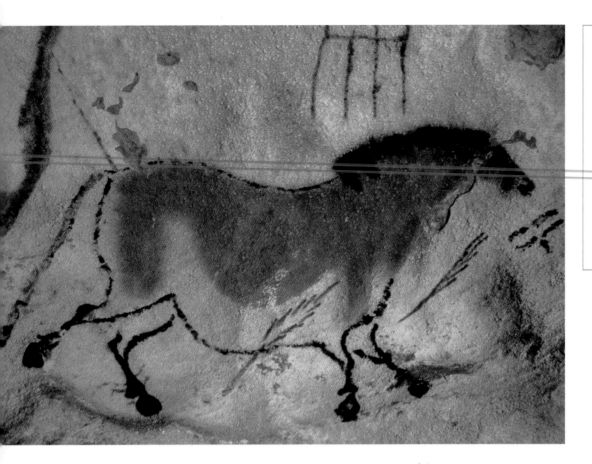

PREHISTORIC
RELIGION

Of our prehistoric ancestors, we know only the bare bones. The clues remain for all to see . . . the cairns and dolmens that dot Ireland, the mighty boulders of Stonehenge, and the sensational cave paintings at Lascaux in France. However, there is nothing to flesh out the assumptions we make about a people and their religion, both long dead. No oral or written tradition remains and excavators of previous decades, who were akin to grave robbers, have taken their toll.

Spirituality cannot be bequeathed to a subsequent age as if it was just a pottery artifact. Historians, both religious and secular, are at a disadvantage. An estimated 50,000 megaliths are scattered over western Europe and northern Africa, while Ireland is particularly rich in megalithic monuments, most of which were built somewhere between 3000 and 2000 B.C. In excess of 300 court cairns have been identified, mostly north of a line running from Galway to Dundalk. On excavation, they were found to contain cremated human bones, round-bottomed "Western Neolithic" pots, flint and chert arrowheads, and the occasional axe or knife. These tombs were probably the centers for local pagan communities of some 50 or so people.

There are also portal tombs, or dolmens, which are above ground and possibly evolved from court cairns. Although their purpose is unclear, they are known as the "dining tables of giants." Massive capstones sit on top of the dolmens, some weighing 100 tons, which may have been hauled into place on wooden rollers.

Passage tombs are usually found in countries bordering the eastern Atlantic, including Portugal, Spain, France, Scandinavia, Wales, Scotland, and, of course, Ireland. They were used for both cremation and burial rituals. Mostly a final resting place for several different generations, some may have been constructed specifically for a great tribal chief. Pottery, carved bone pins, hammer-shaped stone pendants or talismans, and even large balls of chalk have been found inside these tombs. Ireland's most common megalithic monuments are wedge tombs, numbering almost 400, and they are believed to date from the Bronze Age.

STONE LANDMARKS

Twin beliefs in the spirit world and in the power of an ancestor's bones were common. Megalithic landmarks may also have been linked to land rights, while other sacred sites of the era include stone circles, which were probably used for religious gatherings, and stone rows, which appear to have been used for the purposes of astronomy.

Stonehenge is an arresting sight. The prehistoric, massive structure was torn down and rebuilt at some stage during its lifetime, but just how the 80 slabs of bluestone, weighing approximately 26 tons each, were hauled to Salisbury Plain from their source at Preselli in Wales, 130 miles away, and then erected is a mystery. It is no wonder that the splendid construction was thought for years to have been the work of Merlin's magic. Although we don't know its purpose, it is difficult to believe that cloaked Druids, the priestly caste of the Celts, did not carry out religious rituals there, some of which undoubtedly involved human sacrifice. Yet modern historians believe this view was perpetuated in error by overworked imaginations in the 18th and 19th centuries.

LASCAUX

Yet all this seems so recent when compared to the cave paintings at Lascaux. This enormous natural vault was discovered by four boys on September 12, 1940, its walls decorated by the hand of ancient man or men, the fascinating artwork dating from 18,000 B.C. There are bulls, deer, bison, and woolly rhinoceros reverently depicted by the hunters of those distant times. Carefully composed, it is impossible to believe this is randomly drawn age-old graffiti. It must have had a magical or religious significance which has so far escaped our understanding. Michael Jordan, author of *Gods of the Earth*, describes such galleries as "mankind's earliest cathedrals. They defy the norms of architecture and beneath them the human spirit is dwarfed and yet uplifted. They are places of the gods."

Inset below: **Stonehenge, the megalithic structure on Salisbury Plain in England, has enjoyed a complex history. Scientific research indicates it may have been rebuilt three times before 1500 B.C.**

Below: **The Candelabara, drawn centuries ago in the desert sands of South America, is among a series of designs which have prompted theories that early South American people developed manned flights.**

MOTHER GODDESS

Where there is a god, there is a goddess, and she is generally the personification of Mother Earth. To the Egyptians she was Isis, to the Vikings she was Freya. The Canaans knew her as Athirat and the Celts as Nerthus. To the Ashanti she remains Mother Thursday and every week on her name day, workers observe a Sabbath-style ritual of refusing to work on the land.

Like the earth, the Mother Goddess gives life, reveals kindness and cruelty in turn, and is also the taker of life. The significance of the goddess is obvious, reflecting womankind almost perfectly. As women were child-bearers —and early man may not have appreciated the part that he played in the process—they were accorded special honor. Perpetuation of the species was far more crucial in those ancient days than now. So it is easy to imagine that primitive man believed that the world was created by a goddess rather than a god, as later cultures maintained, and consequently the mother goddess figures prominently in most cultures, for a while at least. In fact, many goddesses were worshipped even before male gods came into being.

ICONS OF FERTILITY

One of the earliest traces of the worship of goddesses was found in France on a site known to have been settled by Neanderthals. It was a sculpture carved out of reindeer antler and dating back some 32,000 years according to radiocarbon tests. Its shape was the headless, limbless body of a pregnant or bulbous woman, her chest engraved with mysterious markings. Of course, it may have been just a tribute from a loving husband, but it was the first of many, and the incidence of such models over a broad area implies that its function was a religious one.

Generally, these ancient icons have no feet, legs which are fused together, small or no arms, and, if there is a head, no distinguishable facial features. The emphasis was placed on breasts, abdomen, vulva, and buttocks, for they were carved in times before the present connotations of obscenity or sexuality were put on such objects. Each statuette is now known as a Venus. The patterns that decorate pottery and figurines of later periods are also thought to be indicative of Mother Earth.

A triangle, chevron, or lozenge shape is thought to be the stylized imprint of the vulva and a dot the seed within. Later on, the pregnant goddess became strongly associated with the sow, an animal reminiscent of fertility and rotundity. When gods became eminent, the goddess became an opposing force— for example, mother of the earth against the father of the sky. The moon features largely in goddess worship, not least because women have a menstrual cycle in step with lunar months.

In Africa the Ibo honor the earth spirit Ala, and in the temples devoted to her she is depicted cradling or suckling a child in her arms. Once again this is a common pagan symbol. The cause of Christianity was immeasurably helped among pagans by the picture of the Madonna and Child because it was already a familiar theme to non-Christians. To counter the strong influence of the Mother Goddess came the notion that women were somehow linked with evil. Thus it was broadcast that

" . . . they believe that she intervenes in human affairs and that she rides among their peoples." Tacitus on Nerthus, the Earth Mother of the Germanic tribes.

Eve seduced Adam into tasting forbidden fruit and women were, in many faiths, thought to be a threat to the virtue of the menfolk.

Menstrual blood was deemed by many cultures to be unclean. Zoroastrians, for example, exiled their women to isolated huts every month in order that the males were not tainted with impurity. The mystique of childbirth was dispelled by increasingly sophisticated cultures and, all too soon, the era of the Mother Goddess ended.

Right: **Gross hips and prominent navels emphasized the importance of the icons as fertility symbols.**

Below: **The Mother Goddess cult spread as far as India, as this grey terracotta model, now housed in the National Museum of India, proves.**

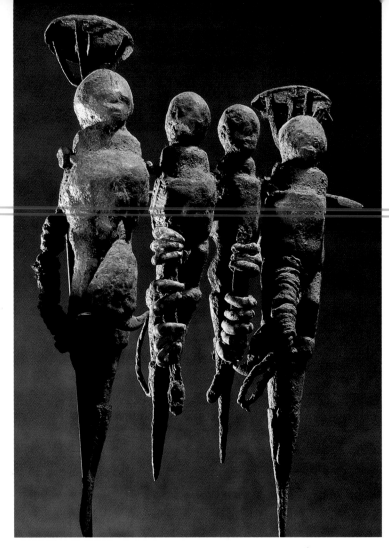

AFRICA

In the middle of the 20th century a tribe in the Southern Sahara, the Dogon, was found to be worshipping a star. To the casual observer there would be nothing new in this, but this was no vast planet that glittered boldly in the night sky. The object of their attentions was Sirius B, invisible to the naked eye and only discovered by the Western world in 1862 with the aid of a powerful telescope. The star is so tiny that it was not photographed until 1970.

WORSHIP OF THE STARS

French anthropologists Marcel Griaule and Germaine Dieterlen discovered the worship when they lived among the Dogon and were further amazed to hear that the tribe knew Sirius B was "the heaviest star" (it possesses enormous density, weighing in at around 20,000 tons per cubic meter) and that it takes 50 years to orbit Sirius, a sister star and the brightest in the sky. Further, from their drawings in the desert sand, Griaule and Dieterlen found out that the natives knew the orbit to be an elliptical one and not circular as they might have thought.

According to the Dogon, they knew about the qualities of Sirius B, which they worshipped alongside Sirius, the Dog Star, thanks to information received from fish-tailed aliens who visited them years before. A strange tale—but then the story of religion contains many.

Further south in central Africa another anthropologist, Jean Pierre Hallet, was equally astonished by the knowledge of astronomy displayed by the Pygmies of the Ituri Forest. They had identified Saturn as Bibi Tiba Abutsiua'ani, "the star of the nine moons," even though the ninth moon was not discovered by Western science until 1899. A tenth has since been detected but, like the others, it is not visible from Earth without the aid of magnification. Like the Dogon, the Ituri have no telescopes. Hallet remarked, "I have never encountered a Bantu or Sudanese who credits Saturn with any moons, much less nine. Most Americans and Europeans are no better informed concerning the existence and number of Saturn's satellites."

It is impossible to know how such tribespeople derived their understanding of astronomy, but these bizarre stories serve to illustrate the driving forces for primitive religions. To the tribespeople the stars, moon, sun, weather, and animal life were relevant forces of life; the dead also have their part to play. And there is no secular side to primitive life. All life is religion.

THE SUPREME BEING

The religious scene in pagan Africa is complex, with thousands of different tribes speaking various languages and holding contrasting beliefs. Like other religions of the undeveloped world, the religious tradition is an oral one and there are no essays or papers to study. Debate about African religion is, therefore, generalized. It appears, however, that most tribes acknowledge a "Supreme Being," although not one that is necessarily involved in human affairs.

In east Africa he is known as Mulungu, in the Congo it is Leza, in the Cameroons Nyambe, while the Yoruba know him as Olorun. Again, the myths surrounding him are many and various, although most have him living in the sky, possibly having thunder as a voice or as an expression of anger. Beneath him often comes an array of lesser gods, nature spirits, or ancestors with whom the tribespeople might hope to communicate.

To these, sacrifices are made and prayers are said. Initiation ceremonies occur for the young and often customs include periods of seclusion and instruction. In some cultures, circumcision is the norm for both boys and girls. Superstition still remains a potent force, with amulets made from a claw, tooth, stone, or shell, often worn to ward off evil spirits and protect against ill health.

AFRICAN RELIGION TODAY

The religion of African tribes is typical of native religions in that the tribesmen cling to the rituals of their forefathers in pursuit of a recognized path to give them some semblance of power in a world full of forces which are outside their control. Witchcraft is feared, but the passions of the people are frequently stirred up by scheming witch-doctors for their own ends.

Such tribes are generally found to the south of the arid continental divide of the Sahara. In North Africa, Islam became established after the conquering Arab armies of the 10th century established communities. Christianity is another success story. For 10 centuries after the arrival of the Muslims, Christianity was confined to the Coptic churches of Egypt and Ethiopia. Today there are something in the region of 160 million Christians of varying sects across Africa. Different regions find the faiths of both Christianity and Islam colored by long-standing local customs.

MASKS

THE WEARING OF MASKS DURING RITUALS IS A STRIKING COMPONENT OF AFRICAN, NATIVE NORTH AMERICAN, AND POLYNESIAN RELIGIONS. THE MAKING OF RITUAL MASKS IS OFTEN DONE IN SECRET TO THE SOUND OF SACRED CHANTS. WHEN THEY ARE WORN, THE MASKS ARE BELIEVED TO ADOPT THE PERSONA OF A SPIRIT WHO WILL UNLEASH ITS POWER ON THE ASSEMBLY. MASK-WEARING BEGAN IN PREHISTORIC TIMES, AS CAVE PAINTINGS HAVE SHOWN. BY DONNING ANIMAL SKINS, HUNTERS HOPED TO MIMIC THE POWERS OF THE BEAST. SO THOSE IN A HORSE HIDE SOUGHT SPEED, WHILE THOSE CLAD IN BEAR FURS ASPIRED TO MIGHTY STRENGTH. MASKS MIGHT BE USED TO RELATE MYTHS AND LEGENDS, FOR EXORCISM OR HEALING, IN FUNERALS OR DURING INITIATION CEREMONIES. SO POWERFUL ARE MASKS THOUGHT TO BE THAT SOMETIMES THEY ARE WORN ON TOP OF THE HEAD TO PROTECT ONLOOKERS. BEFORE TAKING ON A MASK THE WEARER QUIETLY CONTEMPLATES ITS POWER. AFTER USE, THE MASKS ARE EITHER CAREFULLY STORED OR BURNED.

The Native North American might have spoken any one of the 700 different languages that existed from the cold, northerly reaches of Alaska to the steamy southern states. Even now, people believe that no Native American people would be complete without a totem pole—although few know the reason why. In fact totemism is not exclusive to Native Americans, but is found in other tribal societies with a close affinity to nature, such as Australian Aborigines. And just as not all Native Americans lived in tepees—the Iroquois favored long houses—so not every people had a totem pole or were totemic people.

NORTH AMERICA

TOTEMS

Totemism was strongest among the peoples on the northwest coast of North America. A totem pole is a carved monument featuring the sacred plant or animal from which the tribespeople believe they are descended. This plant or animal is said to be a guardian spirit with which the clan has a special bond and is known as a totem. Should the animal be a bear, for example, then bear will not be hunted by those particular people but revered as wise, a protector, and promoter of good health. It is often considered to have astonishing powers, even speech and flight. Totems were strongly associated with men rather than women because of their traditional roles as hunters and warriors.

Totems as guardian spirits are of particular relevance to the shamans who are frequently found in native North American cultures, as well as in Mexico, Siberia, Inuit territories, and northern Asia.

SHAMANISM

A shaman is the bridge between the divine and the earthly, in the mold of priest, healer, wise man, and magician. His *modus operandi* is to fall into a deep trance through repetitive ritual, rhythmic music, or by taking hallucinatory substances such as the peyote cactus or certain

Above left: The Flyer **by the artist John White (c.1570– 1593) depicts a 16th-century shaman.**

Below right: **A painting by Paul Kane (1810– 1871) of a 19th-century medicine mask dance. Belief in the potency of the spiritual power of masks was widespread.**

mushrooms. While the body is inert, the spirit flies to other worlds, with the assistance of his guardian spirit, if he has one, encountering different spirits along the way.

Some may be helpful and are to be encouraged, whereas other spirits are evil and must be fought and defeated. A typical journey for an Inuit shaman takes his wandering spirit beneath the waves to visit the Sea Woman, who might be angered and is therefore withholding catches from the tribe's fishermen. The shaman will negotiate on behalf of his people and perhaps appease her by combing her hair before returning to his body/people.

Another route by which some Native Americans keep in contact with the spirit world is through sweat lodges. A dome-like construction of branches and animal skins with heated stones at its center creates a kind of modern-day sauna, the steam being created by water thrown on the stones. Those inside sweat and the process is considered to be revitalizing and renewing. During his time in the sweat lodge, a Native American is visited by spirits and experience the visions they deliver.

THE GHOST DANCERS

Native Americans live in awe and admiration of their ancestors and it is to these invisible forces that they turn in times of crisis. This explains the rise among the peoples of the Plains and the West in the middle of the 19th century of a cult known as the Ghost Dance religion which promised the return of the dead. It happened when the white settlers were squeezing the Native Americans out of their sacred lands.

To counter the encroachment, Native Americans revived an age-old ritual, the Ghost Dance, which centered on the belief that the world and the white man would soon be swallowed up by a cataclysmic disaster. The Native American, if he continued the Ghost Dance, would escape and live to see the world in its beautiful, natural state, and the return of his ancestors. One of the main inspirations for the Ghost Dance was the visionary Wowoka, who claimed to have seen the future unfolding in terms of the Ghost Dance. He composed songs and taught its principles to Native American peoples, but stopped short of advocating violence against the whites. Frustrated by the continuing oppression, Sioux warriors prepared to take arms against white men and the Ghost Dance was interpreted afterward as hostile. It was made illegal and the U.S. cavalry scoured reservations. During one such sweep against the Miniconjou at Wounded Knee Creek, there was a scuffle, followed by a massacre of Native American men, women, and children. From then onward, the Ghost Dance was laid to rest.

Equally controversial was the Sun Dance. Although details vary, the essence remains the same in that participants dance in a circle for long periods (between two and four days), gazing at the sun. There are periods of fasting, body painting, and contemplation, and the endurance of the dancers is tested by a form of self-mutilation. Each is hooked by a wooden peg in the chest or back to a cordon attached to a central pole. One dancer is hung on the pole until his body weight pulls him free. For the dancers it was an ecstatic experience, but to the white settlers it was barbaric. The Sun Dance was consequently banned by law from the beginning of the 20th century until 1978.

To many, mention of the Aztecs summons up a picture of the terror of doomed captives about to be horribly sacrificed to an unseen god. This method of mass human sacrifice favored by the Aztecs was particularly gruesome. Before his own eyes, the victim's heart would be ripped from his body and offered up while it was still beating.

CENTRAL AND SOUTH AMERICA

However, except for this barbarity, the Aztecs achieved a sophisticated culture which flourished until the arrival of Hernan Cortes and the Spanish Conquistadors in the 16th century.

Mexico had long been settled and civilized, not least by the Chichimecs, Toltecs, and Olmecs, yet the different tribes continued to quarrel amongst themselves. Out of the warring factions the Aztecs emerged, and by the 15th century they controlled the entire region.

APPEASING THE GODS

The reasoning behind human sacrifice was simple enough. Aztecs regularly proffered their own blood, drawn from an earlobe or tongue by a sharpened reed, but the gods were hungry; there could be no better purpose for enemy captives than to offer them up to win spiritual advancement. Religious festivals were held every 20 days and kudos went to those who sacrificed the most valuable objects. In 1487, the Aztec ruler Ahuitzotl had 20,000 captives sacrificed in just four days by eight teams of priests to dedicate the reconstructed temple at Huitzilopochtli.

The souls of the human sacrifices, along with those of warriors killed in battle, were believed to rise to the lofty eastern heavens. The souls of women who died in childbirth rose to the western heavens, heroines for having given the world another Aztec. However, the rest of the population were consigned to a subterranean world of the dead.

Aztecs paid tribute to various gods, one of the most prominent being Quetzalcoatl. Although his name was derived from a bird,

the word is frequently translated as "precious twin" and he is usually portrayed as a plumed serpent. A survivor from the pre-Aztec age, Quetzalcoatl, as God of the Air, was credited with bringing civilization to humans on earth. He was said to have fled in a snakeskin boat, pledging one day to return. When Cortes arrived in boats decorated with feathers, the Aztec king Montezuma initially believed him to be the reincarnated god.

Other Aztec gods included Coatlicue, the Moon Goddess and mother of Quetzalcoatl; Tlaloc, God of Rain; Huitzilopochtli, the "Hummingbird Wizard" and War God, and Tonatiuh, the Sun God; who significantly thirsted for human blood. Each social group

"We, who shudder at the tale of the bloody rites of Ancient Mexico, have seen with our own eyes and in our days civilized nations proceed systematically to the extermination of millions of human beings and to the perfection of weapons capable of annihilating in one second a hundred times more victims than the Aztecs ever sacrificed." Jacques Soustelle

within the Aztec nation forged a special relationship with a particular god, although the general belief was that each was interrelated with the next. One Aztec ruler, concerned at the volume of human offerings that was being made, preached that Tloque Nahuaque was the Supreme God who had no taste for human blood, but his efforts were largely unsuccessful.

AN ORDERED CULTURE

Despite an appetite for human sacrifice, the Aztecs were remarkable for their organization of the cosmos. As with the earlier Mayan culture which was predominant in the Yucatan of Mexico, Guatemala, and Belize between A.D. 300 and 900, the Aztecs imposed combina-

tions of numbers and colors to make sense of their world. There were horizontal and vertical strata, while north, south, east, and west were all numbered. Each sector was assigned gods, priests, military leaders, and other dignitaries. Both peoples had sophisticated measures of time and the Mayan calendar distinguished itself as being one of the most accurate in the whole world.

INCAS

To the south lived the Incas, also victims of Spanish colonialism, who left behind little information about themselves. Incas worshipped the Sun God, Inti, the Creator God, Viracocha or Kon-Tiki, the Rain God, Apu Ilapu, as well as the Moon, Venus, thunder, and the Earth. Viracocha is said to have had three sons, one a trouble-maker who was sent away to rule the underworld, becoming the God of Death and Fertility. The other two represented the conquerors and the conquered.

Like the Aztecs, the Incas were not adverse to the sacrificing of humans. They would take

Left: **These warrior columns or** *Atlantes* **were built by the Toltecs on top of a temple devoted to Quetzalcoatl. It was the Toltecs, dominant between the 10th and 12th centuries, who pioneered worship of Quetzalcoatl in Mexico.**

"Virgins of the Sun," girls aged ten, to the sun temple where some were chosen as wives of the Incas and the rest were offered as sacrifices. A priestess, Coya Pacsa, officiated.

One legacy left by the Incas is the fortified town built in the shadow of the Andean mountain Machu Picchu, discovered by archeologists in 1911. Dating from the 15th century, the town has a plaza, palace, and sun temple built out of large polygonal stones. The Inca empire, with its capital Cuzco, encompassed different peoples who had been overwhelmed by the tribe. Some of those people survived the onslaught of the Spanish Conquistadors and still practice their tamer customs in the recesses of the Andes.

AUSTRALIA

Australian Aborigines have a vivid heritage of ritual and rites, myth and magic. Claims that their religion is the oldest in the world are disputed; nevertheless it is certainly one of the richest and most ancient systems of indigenous beliefs to survive into the 21st century.

STRUGGLING FOR SURVIVAL

It has survived—but only just. Its existence is a tribute to the staying power of the Aborigines who have endured hideous persecution. Like the North American Indians, the Aborigines have fallen victim to the white man's greed and ego. White settlers killed swathes of the population and ensuing waves of white missionaries did their utmost to destroy Aboriginal religion.

The statistics are daunting. A census taken in 1966 registered just 560 non-Christians, out of a population of more than 80,000. Presumably these were the few who were left practicing the faith of their ancestors. More than 50,000 professed to being Christians, while nearly 2,300 listed themselves as having no religion. A mammoth 26,459 did not reply.

In common with other tribal societies, Aborigines set great store by the earth and nature. According to myth, earth was bare until the "totemic ancestors," a divine people, emerged from a deep sleep beneath the crust of the land to form the trees, hills, wildlife, flora, and fauna. Their exit points, including water holes and mysterious caves, became venerated places. These ancestors were capable of assuming animal form and were the root of all life, including human. This was known as the "Dreamtime" or "Dreaming" (Ungud or Wongar). After the creation of earth and life, these supernatural wonders went to ground. Cult objects are devoted to them and rituals are used to invoke them. The Aborigines have a personal totem denoting which plant or animal they are linked to. Those with the same totem are like brothers, and there are vital rituals and responsibilities attached to the totems.

RITES OF PASSAGE

Initiation is a key part of tribal life and only those who have undergone the relevant ceremonies are entitled to take a full part in religious life. The plucking of a tooth is one of the most often recounted, and probably the most significant among boys is circumcision to mark the passage to manhood.

Prior to the ceremony the candidate's body is intricately decorated with paint; afterward there follows several days of instruction. Such ceremonies are now rare. The dismal fate of Aboriginal society is a familiar story. The religion cherished by the Aborigines provided a framework for society, spiritual satisfaction, a welfare system, local laws, and a fundamental pattern of life. Once dismantled, the tribal order fell into disarray.

PERSECUTION

When white settlers arrived in Australia in the late 18th century, there were probably about

300,000 Aborigines peopling some 500 different tribes. Although not instantly hostile to one another, the enmity between white and black began and quickly became entrenched. The whites, offended by the primitive nature of the Aborigines, swallowed up land for farming, mining, and development with no regard for the sacred grounds which the Aborigines revered. Nor were they concerned about the preservation of hunting grounds, consequently starving the aboriginal peoples out of existence.

Unscrupulous whites poisoned water holes and foodstuffs in order to rid themselves of the resident black population. The very presence of the settlers spelled disaster to the Aborigines for with them they brought disease, including cholera and influenza, against which the native people had no defences. As Australia became urbanized, Aborigines were forced to work as farmhands for little or no wages, or driven into the towns and squalid living conditions there. For its part, the government ignored the issue for years and only in 1951 gave its official agreement that Aborigines should be given equality with whites.

Zealous missionaries were kinder but showed no greater respect for the ways and values of the Aborigine. Australian clergyman Richard Johnson considered the Aborigines to be "poor, unenlightened savages," but he was moved to beg his congregation to consider its behavior as an example. "… and if they observe that it is common with you to steal, to break the Sabbath, to be guilty of uncleanliness, drunkenness, and other abominations; how must their minds become prejudiced and their hearts hardened against that pure and holy religion which we profess?"

The missionaries had food and other essentials for which the hard-pressed Aborigine willingly exchanged his religion. These well-meant actions moved Aboriginal poet Kath Walker to question the merit of changing "our sacred myths for your sacred myths."

Above left: **Aborigines have been deprived of their heritage through the incursions of settlers. Aboriginal poet Kath Walker questioned the merit of exchanging one set of sacred myths for another.**

Left: **A celebration dance in about 1843 revealed the body painting skills of the Aborigines whose finishing flourishes were religiously significant symbols.**

'I've watched people die in a cholera hospital in Bengal and witnessed starving children fight for food in Biafra. I have seen people killed and mistreated in Vietnam. But the most emotionally wearing experience of my life has come just in the last few days – among the Aboriginal population of my native land. Now I have seen how we Australians are condemning a whole race of our fellow citizens to short, brutish and miserable lives.' Australian-born Tony Clifton, *Newsweek* correspondent, writing in 1972.

With its close proximity to Australia, it is all too easy to consider the religion of New Zealand's Maoris in tandem with that of the Aborigines. In fact, their beliefs are substantially different. The Maoris owe more to the Polynesian islands of the north rather than to any influence emanating from Australia to the west. Indeed, the Maoris hailed from Polynesia, probably from the Cook Islands, and arrived on the shores of New Zealand by canoe in about 1350.

NEW ZEALAND

MAORI SPIRITS

There is no evidence of the "Dream Time" which plays such an evocative role in Aborigine religion. Instead, there is a series of *atua*, or spirits related to nature, which were borne out of Mother Earth (Papa) and Father Sky (Rangi). For years these parents were in an embrace and their children, living between them, were in darkness. Rather than kill their parents, the offspring decided to separate them. Tu was the Spirit God, Rongo the Spirit of Farming, Turanga the River Spirit, and Tangaroa the Spirit of the Ocean. Most prominent of all was Taane, a victor over the powers of darkness. In the absence of a female, he made the first woman out of Earth and subsequently married her daughter, the Dawn Maiden.

Maoris believe in a supreme being known as Io. Among his hallowed names are Io-take-take, "the foundation of all," Io-roa, "eternal," and Io-mataaho, "glorious one." An argument that Io was fabricated as a response to the encroachment of Christianity has been largely dismissed. It is unlikely that such a whim could infiltrate a secretive and traditional culture such as the Maoris, although it is true that not all peoples were acquainted with Io. Maori beliefs have a tendency to dualism with male/female, earth/sky, or spirit/substance, but lack the prevailing Western obsession with the opposites of good/evil.

TAPU

One of the most significant aspects of the Maori religion is the belief in *tapu*. There is no direct translation but its meaning lies with all that is holy and powerful. To confuse matters further, different tribes have contrasting

"i te kore, ki te poo, ki te as maarama," (Out of the nothingness, into the night, into the world of light), Maori shorthand to explain the Creation.

perceptions of *tapu*, although its nature is invariably broad, long, and deep.

Tapu is encompassing and emanates from the supernatural. It belongs to the earth, water, the moon, sun, and stars because all parts of creation have *tapu*. Sometimes it interchanges with *mana*, loosely translated to spirit power. *Tapu* and *mana* may be diminished, for example when someone becomes a prisoner, although they may later be restored to that person. *Tapu* survives death and Maoris have special restrictions around graveyards to preserve it. When a person is free from *tapu* it is called *noa*.

Priests, of course, were imbued with *tapu* and transferred it to anything they touched. Likewise, a chief had *tapu*, yet so did a dead body. *Tapu* demands respect. To violate *tapu* was to risk grave danger, even death. It was common practice for servants to use long instruments to feed the priests, standing at a respectful distance. In this way, the *tapu* remained unbroken.

SYMBOLISM

Maoris believe that there are three baskets of knowledge. There are many interpretations of this concept between tribes but a general translation follows.

First comes the experience brought to us through our senses. Second comes the understanding of what that empirical experience means, while third is our spiritual proximity to each other and to God brought about through ritual. Great emphasis is placed on the ritual chants here, the *karakia*, to achieve the necessary consciousness.

Commonly found symbols in the *karakia* are the rods, representative pathways, and food. Frequently employed actions are those of loosening away from the destructive and binding to the life-giving. *Karakia* are delivered in a rapid monotone and use traditional language to link up with the ancestors. The major rituals involve birth and children, warfare, the canoe, and death. Legend has it that Taane ascended to the highest heaven to bring back the baskets to earth.

Far left: **A wooden reproduction of the Maori gateway to the underworld.**

Left: **Pendant in the form of the Maori god Hei-Tiki.**

Below: **A war dance by spear-brandishing warriors. Although traditionally they were farmers Maoris fought settlers during the 19th century to protect their lands.**

PACIFIC ISLANDS

Easter Island lies in the South Pacific, just 64 squares miles in size and with a population of around 2,000. Yet this speck in the ocean has long been at the center of an international mystery. Standing like frozen giants along stone terraces there is a series of sculptures which have utterly defied explanation. Each measures 10–40 feet and there are more than 600 in total, all facing west. Many of these *moai* are buried up to their shoulders, leaving eyeless, yellowish-gray faces looming out of the earth. Who put them there, and why, no one knows.

Above: **From Hawaii, a suitably fierce carving of the war god Ku. There is evidence to suggest that human sacrifice once took place upon this chain of more than 20 volcanic islands.**

ISOLATED IDOLS

The island and its statues were first discovered when Dutch Admiral Jacob Roggeveen landed there at Easter in 1722. The British explorer Captain James Cook learned some 50 years later that each 50-ton statue had a personal name and the title *ariki*, which means chief or king. Cook found a disintegrating culture and any clues that the population might have yielded were lost when the majority were rounded up and sent as slaves to Peru. Subsequent inquiries have found that the island, Rapa Nui as it was locally known, became inhabited in about A.D. 400. Although it is 2,485 miles from South America (and 1,243 miles from its nearest neighbor, Pitcairn Island), it is possible that the people originated from there.

A theory by controversial author Erich Von Daniken maintains the artists responsible were extra-terrestrials, stranded for some unknown reason on the remote island.

In 1956 Thor Heyerdahl, the writer and explorer, proved it did not take alien intelligence

to create such works of art. Under his instruction, an eight-strong team created a similar monument using stone tools and softening the volcanic rock with water. Nevertheless, charting the history of religion has once again been frustrated. The stone giants were almost certainly erected for some religious purpose, possibly linked to death and afterlife aspirations.

THE MYTHS OF POLYNESIA

The story of religion in Polynesia, of which Easter Island is a part, is diverse. In Hawaii there was widespread belief in an agricultural god by the name of Lono, a sympathetic figure who sailed across the seas in grief at the death of his wife. He promised to return bearing food. In fact, it was the ill-fated Captain Cook who turned up on the shores and this disappointment on the part of the Hawaiians ultimately led to the death of the explorer.

Another popular mythical hero is Maui, an irreverent scamp who was reared by gods before being installed with a mortal family. He stole fire on behalf of mankind and lassoed the Sun to stop it racing across the sky. Using his grandmother's jawbone as a hook, he fished up whole islands, including New Zealand's North Island. Maui died when he tried to win immortality for man by killing the Goddess of Death. He crawled between her legs and aimed to enter her body, emerging from her mouth and causing her demise. A hitherto trusty bird companion of his roared with laughter at the sight of Maui with his legs dangling from her vagina. The goddess awoke and crushed the adventurer between her legs.

MANA

The life-force of *mana*, similar to that found in Maori culture, prevailed in Polynesia. Chiefs—direct descendants of the gods—possessed it in quantities on behalf of the people. Along with *mana* came *tapu*, now better known in its anglicized form—taboo.

Priests who relied on mediumship as much as ritual led worship at temples. At worst these were the graves of ancestors, but often they were specially constructed and elaborate. There is evidence of human sacrifice taking place in Hawaii, Tahiti, and the Marquesas Islands.

In Micronesia, the northern Pacific islands, there is no evidence of human sacrifice and the worship is directed toward ancestors, not gods. In the southern Melanesia, which includes the islands of New Caledonia and Fiji, the religious scene is once again varied but is dominated by the spirits of nature. Worshippers appeal to the spirits in order to achieve the necessary results of, say, a good harvest or sound health. Should the spirit fail to deliver, then it will be cast off in favor of another. Once again the power of *mana* is essential and it was to increase their own and deplete their enemies' *mana* that the islanders indulged in head-hunting. Cannibalism and, to a lesser degree, human sacrifice were used for similar purposes.

Left: **Explorer Captain James Cook (1728–1779), the man who first charted Australia and New Zealand in his ship Endeavor, was killed in a quarrel with Hawaiians who at first took him to be a returning god.**

CHAPTER TWO
CLASSICAL PAGANISM

If paganism lacked a charismatic founder, then it more than made up for the loss with exotic stories woven around a series of enigmatic gods. Myths and legends helped ancient peoples to make sense of a world which was otherwise beyond comprehension.

Generally speaking, these were the days of animism, the belief that birds, trees, or even stones had souls. Hand-in-hand with animism came fetishism in which particular objects were endowed with magical powers—amulets and charms, for example—and were worshipped. Beyond these early pagan cultures existed anthropomorphism, or the attribution of human features, feelings, and emotions to non-humans. Hence gods were derived from animal worship and were known for being stormy, secretive, forgiving, etc.

The final significant influences on the choice of gods were the cosmic forces of moon, stars, storms, and especially the sun. Perhaps it is not surprising to learn that such beliefs were a fertile breeding ground for magic and super-stition and both became important factors in the beliefs of early cultures.

THE EGYPTIANS

The Pharaohs of Ancient Egypt ranked themselves on a level with the gods. When the Egyptians discovered the art of mummification (preservation of the dead body), the claims of invincibility by the Pharaohs appeared to be proved. So it was only fitting that in death they were treated as royally as they had been in life. All that was needed was a palace for the immortal king.

Above: **Cats were so revered in Ancient Egypt that they were mummified in the manner of kings.**

THE PYRAMIDS

So came about one of the wonders of the world. Exquisitely designed and built, pyramids house the mummified bodies of the Pharaohs, attended in the darkness of the tomb by their servants and surrounded by their worldly goods. Today we interpret the myths surrounding the pyramids as an obsession with death. Perhaps they were better seen as a symbol of a deeply religious civilization with a firm belief in the afterlife.

Each pyramid was constructed as a "house of eternity"—it was built to last. Inside there were hidden tunnels and cavities, and any pyramids not packed with royal possessions were completely empty. This has led to speculation that the pyramids were not really monumental crypts, but objects of supernatural or magical significance. The secret of the pyramids, along with the method by which they were built, has been lost in the desert sands, but most Egyptologists favor the grave theory.

The background to religion in Ancient Egypt is otherwise extensive thanks to the texts inscribed on the walls of tombs, statues, and obelisks, as well as the books which still survive from this time. Outstanding for its contribution to our understanding is the *Book of the Dead*, texts dating from the 16th century B.C. relating to charms and magic formulas set down on papyrus and inserted into mummy cases. Again the theme is frequently death, but perhaps equally worthy literature was devoted to farming or the household yet failed to endure the test of time.

For more than 3,000 years the civilization flourished. Unsurprisingly the number of gods

multiplied during that time, their names and purposes changed, and the religious scene constantly shifted.

THE NATURAL GODS

The principal gods to emerge were Re-Atum, the sun god; Osiris, a king who was betrayed, murdered, and ultimately resurrected; Isis, his devoted sister and wife; and their son Horus, a falcon-god associated with the sky who avenged his father's death.

Not all gods were recognizably human. Some drawings reveal a woman with the head of a lioness or a man with the head of a hawk. These creations probably stemmed from prehis-

toric times when bulls, jackals, and other creatures were ceremoniously buried in the region, pointing to widespread animal worship. Later, live animals were kept in temples, worshipped, and, in death, mummified as a king would be.

The Nile and the Sun were twin forces in the life of the ancient Egyptians, upon which all life depended. Every year the Nile flooded, making islands out of the Egyptian towns. When the waters receded fertile land was left behind, enabling the farmers to grow food and avoid famine.

Mythology explained the floods by claiming that Isis, the mother of all the gods, was weeping for her dead husband Osiris. Strangely, the Nile itself was not deified but was represented by the spirit of Hapy, an abundant figure with a belly, breasts, and a headdress of Nile plants.

Ancient Egypt was divided into 42 districts or *nomes*. Each had its reigning deities and the temples there were often devoted to the local god, although some were built for nationally important gods. Priests served in the temples, but rather than being religious leaders they were more administrators on behalf of the temples, which were the focus of education, land-ownership, and not inconsiderable wealth. Although "out of hours" priests could be married, enjoy sex, and hold down a day job, they were expected to be pure—cleansed with incense, circumcised, shaved of all body hair and manicured—before entering the temple.

Temples were not generally open to ordinary people, who confined their worship to domestic shrines devoted to any god, animal, or symbol that was personally important.

THE GREAT PYRAMID DEVOTED TO CHEOPS STANDS ACROSS 13.1 ACRES AND COMPRISES 2.3 MILLION LIMESTONE BLOCKS, EACH WITH AN AVERAGE WEIGHT OF 2.5 TONS. IT REPRESENTS SUFFICIENT STONE TO BUILT A FOOT-HIGH WALL TWO-THIRDS OF THE WAY AROUND THE GLOBE AT THE EQUATOR—A TOTAL OF 16,600 MILES.

"Who does not know, Vousius, what monsters are revered by demented Egyptians? One part worships the crocodile, another goes in awe of the ibis that feeds on serpents. Elsewhere there shines the golden effigy of the sacred long-tailed monkey." Roman satirist Juvenal.

To both the Greeks and the Romans, religion was a federation of beliefs to which people were only loosely bound. The gods were more human than holy, with egos to be flattered and flaws to be exploited.

THE ANCIENT GREEKS

The stories of the Greek gods were vital and potent, although their influence has been felt more in literature than in religion. However, the stories provided answers which society at the time was seeking. When Roman forces eventually overwhelmed the Greek civilization, many of the deities were adopted by the Empire. Consequently, the gods discussed below have the Roman name in brackets.

THE DIVINE FAMILY

Zeus (Jupiter) was Father of the gods, or supreme deity. Born of Titans, Cronus and Rhea, two of the dozen primeval gods, he eventually vanquished them to establish a new era of deities at Mount Olympus. The sky and the weather were his domain, with thunderbolts his weapon and the eagle his enduring symbol. Zeus, in an early form, was probably introduced into Greece by Hellenic tribes which pushed south into the area around 2000 B.C.

His sister and wife was Hera (Juno), a goddess of womanhood and marriage, strongly associated with the moon. She was driven wild with jealousy as Zeus enjoyed numerous affairs, so she induced a fit of madness in Heracles (Hercules), the son of Zeus by a liaison with a king's daughter, Alcmene. Heracles then killed his wife and children. As punishment he undertook the Twelve Labors, which included killing the Nemean lion, capturing the Cretan bull, and stealing Hera's golden apples away from three nymphs.

There are a further ten members of the upper echelon of gods: Poseidon (Neptune), brother of Zeus and ruler of the sea; Aphrodite (Venus), goddess of love, wife of Hephaestus, lover of Ares and mother of Eros; Artemis (Diana), a nature goddess linked to hunting and fertility born of Zeus and Leto; Athene (Minerva), goddess of war and wisdom who was born from the head of Zeus; Demeter

Left: **Poseidon with Amphitrite, goddess of the sea, painted by Jacob II de Gheyn (1565–1629). She rejected Poseidon's advances and fled to the island of Naxos but was brought back by a dolphin and bore three sons.**

(Ceres) the Earth Mother, sister of Zeus and the mother of Persephone, who was abducted into the underworld by Hades (Pluto); Phoebus (Apollo), twin of Artemis and god of prophecy, poetry, music, and medicine; Hermes (Mercury), son of Zeus and Maia, the youthful winged messenger who invented the lyre; Hephaestus (Vulcan), son of Zeus with Hera, and the blacksmith, or god of fire and volcanoes; Ares (Mars) god of war and Hestia (Vesta), the oldest of the Olympian deities and virginal symbol of hearth and home. The position of Hestia in the top 12 was threatened and finally overwhelmed by Dionysus (Bacchus), god of fruit and wine. A degenerate cult devoted to Bacchus was developed by the Romans and became strongly associated with the decline and fall of the Empire.

REGIONAL WORSHIP

Each god or goddess had sons, daughters, mothers, brothers, or lovers who helped to amplify their character and deeds. Every town or region had a tendency to identify itself with one of the gods: for example, Athene was the patron of Athens, whereas Artemis was strongly linked to Ephesus, where the Temple of Artemis was built in 356 B.C., becoming one of the seven wonders of the world.

The numerous shrines and sanctuaries scattered about the countryside in Greece were not for community worship, but were where, after ritual purification, people might pay respects to the local deity on the implicit understanding that rewards would be forthcoming.

The semi-divine Orpheus was also worshipped, a poet and musician who descended into Hades to retrieve his wife, the nymph Eurydice, who died on their wedding day. He finally lost her by defying the gods and was eventually torn to bits by the menads, the ecstatic female followers of Dionysus. Poetry allegedly written by Orpheus became the theology of the Orphic mysteries. Members of the associated cult were typically vegetarian, highly moral, and entered into mystical rites.

The Greeks were also famed for their complete faith in oracles. Already instituted by the Egyptians, oracles were sacred places where people could ask advice from the deity. Priests would interpret signs to determine the response from the unseen gods.

Oldest among the Greek oracles was the one at Dodana, devoted to Zeus, where the envoy priests listened intently to the rustling of oak trees to discern the relevant messages. The most famous and influential of the oracles during the 6th and 7th centuries B.C. was at Delphi, where the god Apollo announced his responses through a Pythian priestess—her jerks and grunts during intense trances were interpreted by priests.

Clearly, the civilization of the Ancient Greeks was full of superstition. Against this backdrop the philosophers, including Plato and Aristotle, and the mathematician/philosopher Pythagoras found a foothold for their altogether less hysterical views.

Left: The Temple of Fortuna Augusta which stood for just 80 years before being buried in the eruption of Mount Vesuvius. (Reconstruction by Karl Weichardt [1846–1906])

Below left: This silver coin, dating from 235 B.C., has upon it the double profile of Janus, the two-headed Roman god of thresholds after whom the month of January is named.

ROMAN RELIGION

Romans were frequently outraged at the so-called religious rituals they found in parts of their extending empire; for example, they were appalled by the numerous human sacrifices perpetuated by the Celts and the Druids in the name of religion.

A VIOLENT CULTURE

Yet in Rome itself, their pride centered on the Colosseum, a vast amphitheatre built in A.D. 80 which was devoted to the slaughter of animals, criminals, and gladiators who fought to the death, observed by up to 45,000 people. The purpose of the spectacles was a religious one in the eyes of the powerful emperors. They saw themselves as gods or akin to gods; satisfying a lust for blood among the subjects of the empire kept them faithful—it became an opium of the people. This perfectly demonstrates how the rulers of Rome continually used religion for political ends, even after Christianity became a state-sponsored faith.

Between A.D. 106 and 114, some 23,000 people fought for their lives; some of them were Christians, some Jews, but the vast majority were gladiators—prisoners of war, criminals, or adventurers. After training together in schools, they were pitted against one another to fight to the death. Once one fighter lay helpless on the ground it was incumbent upon his opponent to deliver the fatal blow quickly and humanely. Only the "thumbs up" sign from the watching emperor could save the loser.

Roman emperors were tolerant of religions which differed from their own as long as their exalted position was not threatened. This was good news for the polytheistic religions which were able to coexist with the Roman hierarchy, but unfortunate for Christianity and Judaism, both of which insisted that there was one all-powerful God superior to the Roman emperor.

Given the extent of the Empire, it was scarcely surprising that the Romans found themselves presiding over numerous religions and were confronted with a confusing collection of deities. To make sense of the gods which came under their rule, the Romans adapted, adopted, or legitimized the images and icons which they came to know.

NATIVE GODS

However, in addition to the array imported from Greek classical culture, there were other gods that were peculiar to Rome. Saturn was an ancient Italian god and a winter festival was held annually in his honor. His grandson was Faunus, the god of fields and shepherds with the power of prophecy. Quirinus was the original Roman god of war, the celestial form of Romulus, a founder of Rome. Pales was the goddess of cattle and pastures, and Pomona of fruit trees. Flora was the graceful deity of flowers, and Lucina was linked to childbirth.

The Romans also had *numina*, spirits that governed all spheres of life. There was one each assigned to plowing, sowing, harrowing, hoeing, and through every step of the agricultural process to harvesting and storing. It was the same with childbirth, childcare, and other functions that were essential for life. Gradually some of the *numina* took on the status of fully-fledged gods.

There were also the *lares*, spirits associated with ancestors to whom household shrines, the *laraium*, were devoted, as well as the *penates*, guardians of the larder.

From Babylonia came the art of astrology, compelling to some of the Roman dignitaries, while magic and superstition played a large part in the lives of the everyday Roman. Frustrated by the paralysis of society brought on by ludicrous taboos, the intellectual Romans were among the early atheists.

Below: **Mercury, god of commerce and astronomy, painted by Simeon Solomon (1840–1905). He is usually identified by his cap, winged sandals, a staff, and a purse in his hand. In Greek mythology the associated god is Hermes.**

PERSIA

The most influential religion to come out of Persia was the one associated with the prophet Zoroaster (see page 88). In 6 B.C., Zoroastrianism was elevated to become the state religion.

ZOROASTRIANISM

Today it has been largely overshadowed by Islam and Christianity, mostly because Zoroastrians are entirely opposed to the principle of religious conversion.

Yet occasionally we are reminded about the continued devotions of the Zoroastrians. The death of Freddie Mercury, lead singer of the pop group Queen, on November 23, 1991, shot this most reticent of religions into the headlines. His funeral was held in the Zoroastrian tradition as his parents were strict adherents to the faith—although his body was cremated rather than being committed to a Tower of Silence to be left to the mercy of nature.

ZURVANISM

Zurvanism, similar to Zoroastrianism, introduced new identities for existing gods. Ahura Mazda, the benevolent lord of Zoroaster, became Ohrmazd and his evil opponent changed from Angra Mainyu to Ahriman. Governing both was the supreme god of time and space, Zurvan. Within Zurvan was the understanding of procreation, birth, aging, and immortality.

The mythology surrounding Zurvanism was simple: Zurvan longed for a son and waited for a thousand years for him to arrive. Just as he began to doubt he would ever be a father, twins were conceived. Ohrmazd was the personification of good, while Ahriman represented that

moment of doubt. Zurvanism had a fatalistic flavor, while Zoroastrianism preached the existence of free will.

Nothing remains of the Zurvanist movement and religious historians can only speculate about when it existed. It may even just have been part of the Zoroastrian faith.

Although not a Zoroastrian by upbringing, the prophet Mani (A.D. 217–277) was influenced by the faith as well as by the teachings of the Buddha and Jesus. A Christian, Mani had

Left: **Gilgamesh, a Mesopotamian hero, is pictured between two demi-gods in a relief dating from the 9th century B.C.**

Below: **Remains of the city of Ur in Iraq, the home of moon worshippers discovered in 1854 and excavated during the 1920s.**

a divine vision at the age of 12 and was later visited by angels who ordered him to preach the truth about God.

According to Mani, the truth was that there was one God, the Father of Light, who was opposed by the Prince of Darkness—and it is here that Zoroastrianism's duality emerges. From Buddhism came the idea that souls are reincarnated until they can find a release through asceticism into Eternal Paradise.

This new religion became known as Manicheanism and it was imbued with a gentleness inspired by the example of Jesus, whilst other elements encompassed monasteries, monogamy, confession, prayers four-times daily, and non-violence.

Manicheanism became widely persecuted by the Romans and later by the Catholic Church when its mantle was taken up by the heretic Albigenses. Its most famous convert was St. Augustine of Hippo. However, he became a Christian in A.D. 386 and emerged as one of Christianity's great defenders.

Mani (A.D. 216–274) himself was born in Mesopotamia and set out to form a new religion as a young man. Mani's claim was that Jesus, Zoroaster, and Buddha had only expounded fragments of the truth and that he knew the whole story. He was sheltered by the patronage of the monarch Shapur I, but exposed to the enmity of the magi on the death of the king. Mani was captured, interrogated, and died in chains.

THE MYTH OF MITHRAS

Mithraism also came from Persia. It was a kind of secret society, with initiation ceremonies and a mythology all of its own. Mithra was an ancient god who first arrived in the region with the Aryans in 2500 B.C. He defended light, truth, and justice against the forces of evil and sat in judgment on people's souls after death. Mithra fought and killed a cosmic bull whose blood was the source of all animals and plants.

The notion of Mithra was exported, and in the Roman Empire, where he became known as Mithras, an all-male cult sprang up devoted to him. Initiates bathed in the blood of a sacrificed bull and undertook trials of strength as well as pledging to live by a strict moral code. Such machismo appealed to the Imperial soldiers who took Mithras to their hearts and, for a short while, it rivaled Christianity in the Empire. A temple devoted to Mithras was discovered beneath London in 1954.

Still today in Southern Iraq are the minority Gnostic Mandeans, who claim descent from John the Baptist. The soul, they claim, is a spark of light imprisoned in a human form which will only be released at the end of the world. Two key rituals of the Mandeans are baptism, which is often repeated, and the handshake, or *kushta*. Many Mandeans were killed by a plague which struck in the mid-19th century and the survival of the sect is under threat.

Left: **A marble carving central to Mithraism with a winged god, probably Aion, who is surrounded by images recognizable today as the signs of the zodiac.**

The gods of the Vikings have shown remarkable staying power. English-speaking peoples pay tribute to them weekly as Wednesday takes its name from the Norse god Odin, Thursday from his mighty fellow god Thor, and Friday from Frigga, goddess of love, marriage, hearth, and home.

SCANDINAVIAN GODS

For a thousand years the Vikings, or Northmen as they were known, were the scourge of Europe. Renowned warriors, they were as fearsome and unforgiving as their gods. Coming from the cold climates of Sweden, Norway, and Denmark, Northmen were less driven by the sun then by violent weather, such as storms and snow, although they did revere shiny discs representing the sun.

Of course, details of the elaborate mythology which formed their culture changed over the years. For knowledge of Viking beliefs we rely on the information handed down by Christians and this was almost certainly colored. The two primary sources for Scandinavian religion were the Danish scholar Saxo Grammaticus in the 12th century and Snorri Sturluson from Iceland, a century later, who was fascinated by the myths of his forefathers.

The home of the band of the most prominent gods, called the Aesire, was an enormous city fortress called Asgard linked to Midgard or Middle Earth, the human realm, by a rainbow bridge, Bifrost. Three gods were prominent: Odin, Thor, and Frey.

ODIN

Odin, otherwise known as Wotan or Woden, had many facets. He was god of war and lord of the underworld, but was equally famous for his pursuit of knowledge. His thirst for learning was so great that he gave up his right eye in order to drink from the fountain of wisdom. Similarly, he hung himself like a sacrifice on Yggdrasil, the World Tree which spawns occult-style knowledge, with a pierced side in order to master great secrets. Unlikely as it seems, poetry was Odin's passion.

A complex character, he betrayed some of those who pledged loyalty to him by denying them victory in battle. His home was Valhalla which housed all the conquering heroes slain in war. Valhalla, a great hall, had 640 doors, rafters made of shining spears, and a floor covered in shields of gold. The days were filled with feasting and fighting and it was here that the Vikings aspired to go after death. Should they be unfortunate enough to die in their beds, however, the destination was Niflheim, a snowy limbo. It was for this reason that many old or seriously wounded Norse fighters were dramatically killed by their kinsmen, to avoid such indignity. To his admirers, Odin was All-father, or Father of Victory, whereas to his foes he was Ill-doer, Lord of the Gallows, and Terrifier. He was associated with ravens and eagles which became symbols of his presence and power. His steed, Sleipnir, had eight legs, a strange beast which recurs in shaman lore.

Odin had a band of warrior maids, the Valkyries. They were depicted as either great beauties who welcomed the dead from the battlefields into Valhalla, or vicious hags feasting on the blood and dead flesh of slain fighters. His wife was Frigga.

With his strong connection with death the funereal traditions were all devoted to Odin, including the sacrifice of brides, slaves, or maidens at the funerals of lauded Vikings. Like Hindus, they believed both the dead and dying would receive merit by it. Funerals were commonly cremations, often aboard a boat.

THOR

By some accounts Odin's son was Thor, a red-bearded *bon viveur*, although other versions of mythology do not acknowledge any link between these two mighty gods. Thor's trademarks were a powerful stone hammer called Mjollnir, his "girdle of might," which had the magical ability to boost his already considerable strength, and his iron gloves, without which he was not able to raise Mjollnir.

The sound of thunder was made by Thor rumbling about the sky in his goat-drawn chariot. A popular god, he won people's affection by playing jokes on the other gods, although he was quick to anger if mocked by them. Thor was a hero for he defended the gods against their enemies, the giants, and particularly against the World Serpent.

There was a second rank of gods who were closely identified with peace and harvest and these were known as the Vanir. Among them

Above: **The Valkyries, by William T Maud (1865–1903), in helmets and armor, who ride across the battlefield and pluck the bodies of dead warriors in order to carry them to Valhalla where they will live with Odin.**

was Frey, a god of sun, rain, and fertility, who was often represented as a phallus. His twin was Freya, a Venus-like figure who became leader of the Valkyries.

Other key gods include Loki, a shape-shifting mischief-maker, and the benevolent Balder, Odin's son, who was inadvertently killed by Hoder, his blind twin brother.

Norse religion is imbued with a sense of impermanence as the end of the gods and indeed of all mankind was predicted as a doomsday, Ragnarok. On this day the forces of evil, led by Loki, would win against Odin, Thor, and Frey and only two humans, Lif and Lafthrasir, would be left alive.

CHAPTER THREE
JUDAISM

Judaism belongs to the same family of religions as Christianity and Islam. The ethos of each faith is the same, that there is one all-powerful God, the compassionate Creator. Despite age-old conflicts between them, these three different routes to God are remarkably alike. All three demand similar standards of behavior. To each—although for different reasons—Jerusalem is a hallowed city.

Yet the Jewish religion is the parent of the (quarrelsome) siblings, dating back at least 3,000 years. And the feeling of Judaism is different from the other monotheistic religions. More than a system of beliefs, it exudes a sense of identity, a tradition that binds families and fellow Jews together, no matter what. Only this deep-rooted allegiance has kept the faith alive during a history of unprecedented trauma.

THE PATRIARCHS

God's work had just begun when he created Heaven and earth, water, birds, and animals and, on the sixth day, man and woman. The man was Adam, the woman Eve, and together they fell from grace when they succumbed to temptation offered by the crafty serpent. Their punishment was hard work for men, painful childbearing for women, and, ultimately, death for all.

THE FLOOD

One of Adam and Eve's sons, Cain, subsequently killed his brother, Abel. Nevertheless, the dynasty flourished although its people were famously wicked and violent. God administered his punishment ruthlessly. He told the only righteous man alive, Noah, to build an ark and take on board his family and at least one pair of all the animals in the world. Then the flood came. It rained for 40 days and nights and the water destroyed all living things except those on Noah's ark. Finally the flood subsided and the ark came to rest on the mountains of Ararat. All the world's population can trace their line back to Noah, the grandson of Methuselah who died in the year of the flood at the age of 969 years.

To Christians this is the Old Testament, to Jews it is the Hebrew Bible which begins with the Torah or "the teaching." Jews believe these were the words of God imparted to Moses on Mount Sinai. Great store is set by Torah's words, so much so that the Jews are often called "the people of the Book." It is an epic story of drama and divinity upon which the faith is founded.

Stories of a devastating flood in the earliest years of history also appear in other traditions as far flung as the native peoples of Ontario, the Hindus of India, Icelanders, Maoris, and

Above: **Mosaic showing Noah taking a pair of every species into his ark to escape the ravages of the flood.**

Right: **The murderous Cain attacks his brother Abel, showing the evil men can do (Jacop Nehretti Brudermord [1544–1628]).**

African pygmies. (Despite the efforts of archeologists, no conclusive proof has been found to indicate that a great flood occurred worldwide, although climatic calamities on a local scale are accepted even by sceptical geologists.)

So God not only bestows favors but also wreaks vengeance. In the Hebrew Bible God is remote, righteous, and awesome. It is a far more mellow God who is described in later Christian and Islamic writings.

ABRAHAM

Abram was a good and wealthy man, a descendant of Noah's son Shem, who lived with his wife Sarai and nephew Lot in Ur, the great city of Babylonia. Abram lived in about 1700 B.C. and was the first of the Patriarchs who feature so prominently in the Jewish faith.

At the instigation of Abram's father Terah, an idol-maker, the family left Ur to follow a nomadic life. God urged Abram to go to Canaan where he would found a great nation. God promised he would be known as Abraham (the father of multitudes). To Abram and his wife Sarai, who were growing old and were unable to have children, this must have seemed an impossible dream, yet Abram did as he was bid. Sarai urged Abram to father a child by her Egyptian maid Hagar and so Ishmael was born, destined to figure prominently in Islam's history.

It was not until he was 99 years old that Abram and his wife produced their own child, a son called Isaac. Abraham's most painful

ABRAHAM WAS RENOWNED FOR HIS HOSPITALITY. SO GREAT WAS HIS LOVE OF MAN THAT HE STOOD BY THE DOOR OF HIS TENT TO URGE GUESTS INSIDE. EVEN TODAY RABBIS POINT TO ABRAHAM AS AN EXAMPLE FOR JEWS TO FOLLOW AND BY TRADITION EVERYONE IS WELCOME AT THE DINNER TABLE, PARTICULARLY FOR FESTIVE MEALS.

moment came when God commanded him to sacrifice Isaac. Father and son went up into the mountains where Abraham prepared the altar, built a pyre, bound up his son, and was about to wield the knife to kill the boy when God's angel intervened. Abraham had not flinched, such was his faith in the will of God. To reward such unquestioning loyalty God made a covenant with Abraham: "Because you have done this and have not withheld your son, your favored one, I will bestow my blessing upon you and make your descendants as numerous as the stars of heaven." The sign of the covenant was to be the circumcision of Abraham and Isaac, a practice which continues to carried out on all Jewish boys when they are eight days old.

Abraham arranged a marriage for Isaac to a cousin Rebekah who would give birth to Jacob and Esau. Abraham died aged 175 and was buried with his wife Sarah. Jacob fathered 12 sons who became the leaders of the dozen different tribes of Israel.

Few mothers can read the story of Moses without feeling a pang of sisterly compassion. The Hebrew woman, Jochebed, gave birth to a fine healthy boy in Egypt just as the Pharaoh had ordered all male Israelite babies to be killed.

BABY IN THE BULRUSHES

She left Moses in a watertight basket made from bulrushes in the shallows of the Nile. A short distance away the baby's sister Miriam waited and watched. She saw the Pharaoh's daughter come down to the river to bathe and when the noblewoman found Moses, she took

pity upon the helpless baby who was so obviously a doomed Israelite child. Miriam seized her moment. She dashed down, offering to help the Pharaoh's daughter find an Israelite wet nurse to care for the baby. Moments later she produced Jochebed and, unbeknownst to the Egyptian onlookers, the mother and her son were reunited.

The dramatic events following his birth in 1593 B.C. were merely preparation for Moses' later years when he was chosen by God to lead the Israelites out of slavery in Egypt to the promised land and freedom. For much of his life, Moses was a humble shepherd—until God spoke to him through a burning bush, calling on him to free his people from Egypt.

EXODUS

With his brother Aaron, Moses confronted the Pharaoh, asking him to let the Israelites go. When the purpose of his mission was denied time and again, Moses, with God's help, instigated 10 plagues, the first turning all the waters of the Nile into blood. Then came frogs, lice, flies, cattle disease, boils, hail, locusts, and darkness, while the last was the most terrible, the death of every Egyptian first-born.

OUT OF AFRICA

The Pharaoh finally acquiesced and the Israelites left Egypt. Although the Egyptian army was in hot pursuit, Moses saved his followers by parting the waters of the Dead Sea, leading his people across and leaving the waves to crash down on the Egyptians.

If Moses thought his problems were over, he was disappointed. The journey to the Promised Land was arduous and he was plagued by the endless complaints of the Israelites who were concerned about food, shelter, the future, the past, and so forth. There were even attempted coups to remove Moses from power. Although a vessel of God's power, Moses felt himself to be a weak man. He was also over 80 when he

Above: **Moses receives the Ten Commandments, from an illustration in the 12th-century Winchester Bible.**

Opposite top: **Moses and his brother Aaron lead the Exodus of Israelites from Eygpt with armed guards in hot pursuit.**

went to Egypt to free the slaves. Through an outburst of anger Moses lost the opportunity to enter the Promised Land. God was unrelenting and condemned him to die in the desert.

THE WORD OF GOD

Moses received the "Ten Commandments" on Mount Sinai and carved them onto stone tablets which were placed in an Ark. The Ark accompanied the Hebrew people on their wanderings until it finally came to rest in the Temple in Jerusalem and vanished in about the 6th century B.C. The Commandments in Exodus are followed by other statements on conduct which separate the Old Testament God from the New. "Wherever hurt is done, you shall give life for life, eye for eye, tooth for tooth . . ." as opposed to the "turn the other cheek" philosophy that Jesus later preached. Changing times clearly produced different Biblical theories.

For years it was accepted that, at God's bidding, Moses wrote the first five books of the Hebrew Bible—Genesis, Exodus, Leviticus, Numbers, and Deuteronomy—collectively known as the Pentateuch. Doubt has recently been cast on this theory with corroboration from independent sources of some of the incidents that took place, dating it after Moses's death on Mount Nebo, east of the Dead Sea.

THE TEN COMMANDMENTS
(from The New English Bible)
—You shall have no other god to set against me.
—You shall not make a carved image for yourself nor the likeness of anything in the heavens above or on the earth below or in the waters under the earth. You shall not bow down to them or worship them; for I, the Lord your God, am a jealous god.
—You shall not make wrong use of the name of the Lord your God; the Lord will not leave unpunished the man who misuses his name.
—Remember to keep the Sabbath day holy.
—Honor your father and your mother.
—You shall not commit murder.
—You shall not commit adultery.
—You shall not steal.
—You shall not give false evidence against your neighbor.
—You shall not covet your neighbor's house . . . or anything that belongs to him.

After the Torah comes the second of three sections of the Hebrew Bible, the Prophets or Nevi'im. Although these are words of stature they lack the sanctity of the Torah.

Nevi'im is divided into eight books, probably the oldest detailed narratives known to mankind, which focus on the Former Prophets—Joshua, Judges, Samuel, and Kings—and the Latter Prophets—Isiah, Jeremiah, and Ezekiel.

MOSES'S LEGACY

On the death of Moses, his successor Joshua led the Hebrew people into Canaan, the Promised Land, which he divided up between the 12 tribes of Israel.

The country continued to develop, peopled by characters like Deborah, the prophetess and warrior, Samson, scourge of the Philistines whose strength was sapped when his mistress Delilah cut off his hair, and Ruth, who so loved

THE PROPHETS

her widowed mother-in-law that she left her own people to live in Bethlehem.

Israel was at war with surrounding tribes, but these troubled times were temporarily curtailed by Samuel who, reluctantly, united the differences of the country under the strong leadership of a monarch. Samuel was a prophet raised by a priest in the 11th century B.C. A formidable fighter, he was also shrewd enough to realize that his sons would not be worthy successors. At the insistence of the people and with the approval of God, Samuel set about finding a king for Israel. When the lowly Saul of the Benjamin tribe appeared searching for his father's lost donkeys Samuel was told by God that this was the future king.

SAUL V. DAVID

Saul was duly anointed and he, like Samuel, was a warrior, as was his son Jonathan. Unfortunately, he lost Samuel's confidence and God's

favor. David, a shepherd, was anointed by Samuel although Saul remained on the throne. It was not for his skills as a harpist that David is remembered, but for his victory over Goliath, the nine-foot tall champion of the Philistines.

Jealous of his rival, Saul tried unsuccessfully to kill David and eventually killed himself by falling on his sword after being cornered in battle, once more fighting the Philistines.

David now became king. Although his personal life was vivid—he seduced Bathsheba, the wife of one of his generals, and then had the man killed so he could marry her—David was a talented leader of men whose reign was generally thought to be prosperous.

His successor was Solomon, David's son by Bathsheba. Given the gift of wisdom by God, he became famous for his judgment in a dispute among two women over a baby. Both claimed to be its mother so Solomon suggested the child should be cut in half. One woman

"Hear, O Israel, the Lord our God is one. And you shall love the Lord thy God with all thy heart and with all thy soul and with all thy might." *Shema*, the confession of faith recited twice daily by Jews.

agreed while the other said she would relinquish her claim rather than kill the infant. Solomon realised this was the real mother.

THE FALL OF ISRAEL

However, Solomon's wisdom failed him where women were concerned. He gathered an estimated 700 wives, many from other countries, and 300 concubines. Solomon adopted their idolatrous habits, for which God punished him by dividing up his kingdom.

His son Rehoboam was consequently unable to keep the kingdom of Israel intact. It was reduced to an area in the north while the south became the kingdom of Judah.

Paganism encroached on Israel once more, notably during the reign of Ahab, the seventh king, and his wife Jezebel. This was also the era of Elijah who performed many miracles during his lifetime, as did his successor Elisha.

Israel and Judah continued to stray from the path of God and ultimately the kingdoms were punished by being overrun by the Assyrians and the Babylonians in a period known as "the exile." There were three prophets whose life and times are related in the Old Testament, Isiah, Jeremiah, and Ezekiel, with a further 12 "minor" prophets, among them Hosea and Malachi, all responsible for relaying God's message to the Israelites. They all saw the hopelessness of Israel's cause.

AWAITING A SAVIOUR

Jeremiah declared that the covenant made between God and Abraham had been broken. The prophets looked beyond the disaster to see a time when God would intervene to repair the damage; others pinned their hopes on a Messiah who would come to earth bearing God's message. Christians have identified Jesus as the Messiah, while the Jews are still awaiting his arrival. It is this hope that sustained the Jews during waves of persecution, although today there is less emphasis on the coming of the Messiah and more laid on the dawning of a new era of peace and prosperity.

The third section of the Hebrew Bible is the "Writings," or *Ketubim*, which include the Psalms, Proverbs, Job, The Song of Songs, Ruth, Ecclesiastes, Esther, and Daniel.

ISRAEL

In the 6th century B.C. Babylonian invaders laid to waste much of Jerusalem, Judah, and Israel. Jewish people were forcibly removed from the Promised Land to which Moses had led them. Generations came and went but the dream of Israel, the Jewish Holy Land, remained alive.

Jewish hero Judah Maccabee and his brothers resurrected the aspirations of the Israelites when they led a successful revolt against Syrian rulers of Jerusalem. The temple, which had been desecrated, was restored to the Jewish faith once more, but the liberation was short-lived. By 63 B.C., just 100 years after the death of Maccabee, the Roman Empire swallowed up Israel in its inexorable spread.

We know from the New Testament Gospels about the Roman influence on the daily lives of the Jews in the Holy Land, although there were laws to protect Jewish worship. An uprising by the Jews in A.D. 70 was ruthlessly crushed, the penalty being the destruction of their second

Temple. Within 70 years the Romans expelled the Jews from their homeland.

A NATIONLESS PEOPLE

It was now the fate of the Jewish people to roam the world making a home where they could. This exodus by the Jews is called the *Diaspora*, a Greek word meaning dispersion. It began with the Babylonian invasion of Israel, but accelerated after the 1st century when Jews were ousted by the Romans.

From Israel, they went through North Africa to Morocco and then over to Spain, to France, and England. Jews of Spanish origin became known as the *Sephardim*, derived from *Sepharad*, the Hebrew word for Spain.

Others sought refuge in Constantinople, traveling from there to Italy and Germany. Germanic Jews were called *Ashkenazim*. Israel was absorbed into the area know as Palestine and was ruled by a number of different monarchs and emperors.

The history of the Jewish people was a troubled one. It was not until the middle of the 19th century that the Jewish nationalist movement made itself volubly heard and was formally launched at the First Zionist Congress held in Basle in 1897 (Zion being the name of a hill in Jerusalem). For the first time in centuries the desire of the Jews for a national homeland was voiced in the international arena. Behind the thrust of Zionism was, among others, Theodor Herzl (1860–1904), a Hungarian-born journalist and playwright who went on to become the first president of the World Zionist Organisation, a product of the 1897 Congress. A Jewish National Fund was established in 1901 to buy land in Palestine.

At last Jews began drifting back to the land of their forefathers. Tel Aviv was founded in 1909 to house a booming Jewish population. Hopes were high after the Balfour Declaration of 1917 when Arthur Balfour, British Foreign

Secretary, pledged aid for the establishment of a national Jewish homeland in Palestine—well-intentioned, but doomed to failure. Arabs in the area were unconvinced by British assurances that their status would be maintained, while many Jews were wary of cooperating with Britain, a colonial power. The Balfour Declaration was finally abandoned in 1939.

THE HOMECOMING

After the Holocaust, in which European Jewry was decimated during World War II, the Zionist dream became a reality. Israel was created in 1948 as a homeland and a safe haven for the world's Jews. Its history has not been without incident. In fact, troubles began with its unhappy Arab neighbors almost immediately. Attempts to reach a peaceful and amicable settlement in the region still continue today.

There are 6,000,000 Jews living in Israel, some 25 per cent of the world's Jewish population. Many more Jews live in the United States which plays a dominant role in Jewish affairs. Still the effects of the *Diaspora* are felt today, with Jews living as minorities in Great Britain, France, Canada, Argentina, Brazil, South Africa, and many other countries. Nicholas de Lange, author of *Judaism*, puts it like this: "They are a small people with a strong sense of their own importance and destiny; a scattered people with a strong sense of unity; an urban people whose religion still bears many traces of a rural past; an ancient people whose roots are generally not in the place where they currently live."

Above left: **A view over Tel Aviv, founded in 1909 to house the burgeoning Jewish population in the region.**

TORAH AND TALMUD

A brief survey of the Old Testament is enough to confirm that the old and respected texts throw up more questions than they answer. To a Jew the quest to know the Torah and its meanings begins in boyhood and never ends. One verse in the Ethics of the Fathers sums up the Jewish attitude to the Bible: "Turn it, and turn it, for everything is in it; contemplate it, and grow old and gray over it, and do not stir from it. You can follow no better course than this."

To a Gentile or non-Jew the prospect of learning the "Pentateuch," the first five books of the Old Testament, and all the hidden messages wihtin them, is daunting. But there is much more to know than that. For alongside the written laws there is a rich oral tradition, the *Talmud*, which holds just as much authority.

THE TALMUD
The *Talmud* comprises two different forms of writing: the first is the *Mishnah*, the oral tradition which was committed to paper in about

A.D. 200 following the martyrdom of Rabbi Akiba, an inspired teacher of the day. It was eventually marshaled into six sections, each dealing with different aspects of life. There was one each for agriculture, festival days, marriages and divorce, the law, Temple sacrifice, and ritual purification.

Subsequently, there was all manner of debate, so a commentary—and then a commentary on that commentary—was drawn up; it is known as the *Gemara*. There was no single contributor, but a host of writers responsible for the works over many years. The collected teachings of generations of rabbis was at last safe for posterity.

There are two *Talmuds*, one from Babylonia and the other from Palestine. The first, being three times longer than the second, is generally considered the most authoritative. Both are written in a mixture of Hebrew and Aramaic.

Attempts to codify the contents of the *Talmuds* to make them less academic and more accessible have been made over the years. Maimonides produced just such a work, although it was widely criticised when first seen because he had deleted so many references.

Jewish theology is also preserved in the *responsa*, replies to questions on the Bible given by scholars and religious leaders between the 6th and 11th centuries. There is also the *Midrash*, a compilation of homilies gathered over the centuries.

KABBALAH

Another largely medieval development in Judaism was the Kabbalah (Cabalah or Qabbalah), a mystical tradition handed down from teacher to pupil which helped the student to find unity with God. Legend has it that God taught the Kabbalah to the angels, who in turn enlightened Adam so that he might find his way back to God. It was known by Noah, Abraham, and Moses who initiated 70 elders.

The primary book of Kabbalism is the *Sefer ha-Zohar* or "Book of Splendor," written between 1280 and 1286 by Moses de Leon in Spain, the heart of anti-Maimonides country.

To achieve union with God, the book suggests elevation through a path which is represented on the Tree of Life. The "fruits" of the Tree, the *sephirot*, of which there are ten, symbolize the attainment of knowledge.

There are seven *sephirot* in the base of the tree. They are sovereignty, foundation, endurance, majesty, beauty, loving-kindness, and judgment. All correspond with energy centers along the spine. The top three are understanding, wisdom, and crown or humility. Kabbalism extends far beyond this outline explanation and takes years to master. Popular between 1500 and 1800, interest in it has since declined, although its impact on Jewish folklore was substantial. The Kabbalah was borrowed by Western occultists to form part of ritual magical texts.

"If the Bible is the cornerstone of Judaism then the Talmud is the central pillar, soaring up from the foundations and supporting the entire spiritual and intellectual edifice . . . No other work has had a comparable influence on the theory and practice of Jewish life." Rabbi Adin Steinsaltz

JEWISH LAW

From this enormous array of literature is drawn the *halakhah*, Jewish law encompassing everything from criminal and civil law to morals and ethics. It is over attitudes to the *halakhah* that the Jewish faith split.

Orthodox Jews accept the law and rabbinical authority. In the 18th century, however, Liberal Judaism arose in Europe to question age-old traditions and encourage constructive criticism of the *Torah* and *Talmud*. It was given continuity by Reform or Progressive Judaism which plays down elements like the expectation of a Messiah and the desire to return to the Holy Land. Reform Jews offer equal opportunities to women during worship, while worshippers in the Orthodox synagogues are separated by sex. Conservative Jews steer a middle course. There are also Hasidic Jews, those who try to reach God through ecstatic prayer.

Faith is a matter of the heart rather than the head. Without exception the world's religions are based on a tradition of mysticism. To be a believer means to suspend cold, hard reality, for a while at least.

Rationalists who like to chip away at the fascia of religion are rewarded with small victories. Although they have yet to convince significant masses of population that all religion is an elaborate hoax, they can, with a few carefully chosen facts, undermine the claims of the scriptures or holy men.

MAIMONIDES'S PRINCIPLES

Right: A statue of Maimonides in his birth place, Cordoba, Spain. The great thinker and writer was hounded by Jews and Gentiles alike yet his controversial views have since become enmeshed into Judaism.

RATIONALISING REVELATION

Each faith has its thinkers to bridge the gap between religion and rationalism. In Judaism the most eminent is Moses Maimonides (1135–1204), also referred to as Rambam.

Born Moseh ben Maymun in Cordoba in Spain, he was driven out by the persecution of Jews inspired by Muslim fundamentalists. In 1165 he and his family departed for Morocco and then on to Cairo, where he eventually became physician to Sultan Saladin.

Mainmonides's intention was to marry the Aristotelian rationalism of the day with Jewish revelation, putting Judaism onto a firm philosophical footing. He failed to foresee the consequences which would, ultimately, engulf the Jewish world. Retrospectively he was he declared, although he found the case that the world was eternal and not created unproved.

SEEKING THE KING

He used the following parable to illustrate his points of view. "God," he declared, "was like a king in his palace and his subjects were trying to find him. Those who merely obeyed the Torah had not even set eyes on the palace. Those who read the *Talmud* but failed to apply reason to their faith were walking outside the palace walls. It was the faithful who read and understood philosophy that won access to the palace antechamber—and only when they understood the limit of what can be learned did they enter the palace itself."

considered one of the greatest Jewish philosophers to have ever lived.

Maimonides wrote three definitive works: a commentary on the *Mishnah*, the law passed down orally through generations; the *Mishnah Torah* or "Second Torah" which investigates further the Torah and all its implications; and, lastly, the *Moreh Nevukhim* or "Guide for the Perplexed" harmonizing Jewish teachings with philosophical thought.

His aim was to unify the Jews under one intellectually sound code. In practice his writings split communities with his "Guide for the Perplexed" being burned in the streets of France. Dogmatic Jews were outraged by what they considered to be heretical views.

For Maimonides his belief in the power of reason was balanced by his unshakeable faith in Moses and God. Yes, he believed that people did talk with God, but that the encounters took place not literally but in a dream. Anyone who was mentally prepared could receive prophecies,

"We are obligated to love every single fellow Jew as ourselves, as the Torah states, 'Love your fellow man as yourself.' [*Leviticus 19:18*] Therefore, we must praise others, and we must care about their money just as we care about our own money and our own dignity."
Mishne Torah – Maimonides.

THE SYNAGOGUE

For years the center of Jewish religious life had been the Temple in Jerusalem. When this was destroyed in 587 B.C. and the Jewish people deported to Babylon, they were deprived of an important religious focus.

The prophet Jeremiah, still imprisoned in the ruins of Jerusalem, urged them by letter on God's behalf: ". . .seek the welfare of the city where I have sent you into exile and pray to God on its behalf, for in its welfare you will find your welfare."

THE GATHERING

Accordingly, people gathered together in the houses of prophets or community elders to pray for themselves and their captors and this was the antecedent of the synagogue. The original meaning of the word was "gathering" and it was probably drawn from the Greek word *synagein*, to gather together. Only later did it change from being a verb to a noun.

Having done so the synagogue became a familiar feature of every village and town. By the time of Jesus, the Gospels reveal, there were synagogues in everyday use. When the Temple in Jerusalem was destroyed for a second time in A.D. 70. the vacuum was filled by the synagogue.

CENTERS OF THE COMMUNITY

At the time synagogues were radical. For the first time people were drawn together not for sacrifice or rites and rituals, but for congregational prayer and instruction. Remember that this was before churches or mosques were created. Synagogues have always been much more than just venues for prayer.

Another function—perhaps even the primary one—is education, particularly for study of the *Torah*. This was important in times and places where education was the preserve of the elite, and was therefore denied to Jewish children who too frequently populated the lower orders. Nowadays the synagogue is likely to provide classes in Hebrew, once again for a better understanding of the *Torah*, as well as being a center of Jewish culture. In its role as a community center, there might be youth groups, women's groups, and sports activities on offer, too. From the synagogue comes the interpretation of Jewish law on civil matters, such as divorce. It might be the licencing authority in Jewish matters: for example, inspecting the premises of a local butcher who wishes to sell kosher food.

In the past synagogues acted as bakeries, to provide unleavened bread for the Passover celebrations, and even as hostels.

INSIDE THE SYNAGOGUE

Older synagogues would be furnished with a *mikvah*, or ritual bath, for the worshipper who was unable to find another place to bathe. These days, with modern facilities freely available, *mikvahs* have fallen into disuse.

Synagogues are of a simple rectangular design. The end that faces Jerusalem houses the Ark or closet in which the scrolls of the *Torah* are kept. A curtain usually shields the Ark from the rest of the building to define the area as a holy sanctuary and there is a "perpetual light" which burns before it, reminiscent of the Temple in Jerusalem. Although there is a

Left: Jerusalem's Temple was first destroyed in 587 B.C. signaling the start of the synagogue. The Temple was rebuilt only to be destroyed a second time by the Romans.

Above: **An 18th century depiction of the blowing of the Ram's Horn. This is sounded on Rosh Hashanah, the Jewish New Year. It symbolizes Abraham's sacrifice of a Ram, whose horns were entangled in a thicket, before binding Isaac to the altar.**

pulpit from which readings are made, the altar, which is central in the Christian church, is absent. Such is the modesty of the synagogue that there is no other regalia except a reading desk, emphasizing the characteristic love of reading and books among Jewish people.

Seats are on two or three sides facing toward the Ark. In Orthodox synagogues there is often a gallery for women and children, a reminder of when they were once positioned behind a screen.

Jewish people have long been uncomfortable with the notion that prayers should be said at a specific time in a set place. There is a question mark in many people's minds over the value and sincerity of such mechanical prayers. So the home is equally as important for worship as the synagogue, and many festivals and celebrations are centered there.

CELEBRATIONS

The Jewish Sabbath is more than just a day of rest. Beginning on Friday evening at sunset and ending on Saturday at nightfall, the Sabbath has three aspects: a day of rest, a day of holiness, and a day of gladness.

Of course, the inspiration for the Sabbath came in the Ten Commandments. In full it instructed, "Remember to keep the Sabbath day holy. You have six days to labor and do all your work. But the seventh day is a Sabbath of the Lord your God; that day you shall not do any work, you, your son or your daughter, your slave or your slave-girl, your cattle, or the alien within your gates; for in six days the Lord made heaven and earth, the sea, and all that is in them, and on the seventh day he rested."

BAR MITZVAH

Consequently there are specific rules about what may and may not be undertaken on the Sabbath. It is an inappropriate day for public mourning and all mention of sad events is erased from the prayers. There are special services at the synagogue and meals at home; it is a weekly renewal of the covenant between God and the Jewish people. It will be on the Sabbath following his 13th birthday that a Jewish boy marks the advent of his religious duty with a Bar Mitzvah. On this day he is called for the first time to read publicly from the *Torah* and he becomes a fully fledged member of the congregation. Afterward he may wear the *tefellin*, a black leather box which contains strips of parchment on which is inscribed four sections of the "Pentateuch." They are worn on the arm and forehead during morning prayers although not usually on the Sabbath or during festivals.

At the age of 12 girls may have a Bat Mitzvah with a celebration in the synagogue or at home. However, such celebrations are still not as widespread as Bar Mitzvahs.

THE KOSHER DIET

Jews also observe the law laid down by God about food. The rules regarding which animals can be killed, how they are killed, where the carcasses are kept, and how they are cooked are strictly followed. In short, pig is completely off the menu as it is regarded as unclean. Dead animals have to be drained of blood, or *kashered*, and must be kept away from dairy foods. After eating meat, Jews must wait four to six hours before consuming milk, cheese, or other dairy products.

Food is also of great importance when it comes to Jewish festivals. Passover, or Pesach, commemorates the flight from Egypt. The Hebrews marked their doors with the blood of a lamb so that God would pass over them when he brought about the final plague.

Central to the celebration is the Seder, a plate of food made up of three matzo crackers, a roasted shank bone, an egg, sprigs of parsley, bitter herbs (such as horseradish) and *haroset*, a mixture of apples, nuts, cinnamon, and wine. All the items are symbolic. The lamb bone—which is not eaten—represents the Passover lamb. The egg is also left untouched

as it is a token of spring and new life. The parsley, dipped in salt water or vinegar, is a reminder of the tears of the Hebrew slaves and the salt of the sea, and the horseradish is for the bitterness of slavery. Haroset is eaten with the herbs and symbolizes the bondage the Hebrews endured. There is an empty cup on the table, awaiting the prophet Elijah who, according to the Book of Malachi, will arrive before the day of redemption.

Other festivals include:

Hannukah—An eight-day festival of lights marking the re-dedication of the Temple in Jerusalem in 165 B.C. after it was won back from the Syrian Greeks by Judas Maccabeus and his men.

Purim—This is a celebration marking Esther's triumph over the Jew-hating Haman in Persia. It is seen as a time for exchanging gifts and carnival parades.

Rosh Hashanah—The Jewish New Year upon which the ram's horn, or *shofar*, is sounded in the synagogue.

Shavuot—A two-day celebration which marks the giving of the "Ten Commandments." It is also called the Feast of Weeks.

Sukkot—This is otherwise known as the Feast of Booths; it is a thanksgiving for God's protection of Moses and the Hebrews who spent 40 years in the wilderness. Some Jews construct commemorative shacks from branches to eat in as a reminder of the poverty of their forefathers.

Tisha B'Av—A day of remembrance for the destruction of the Temple in Jerusalem by the Roman Emporer Titus in A.D. 70.

Yom Kippur—Historically, this is a day of atonement when Jews fast for about 25 hours, reflect on their sins, repent, and seek forgiveness from God.

> THE JEWISH CALENDAR IS MOON-BASED, UNLIKE THE SOLAR-INFLUENCED GREGORIAN CALENDAR, AND BEGINS IN THE AUTUMN. TO KEEP IN STEP WITH THE SEASONS THE JEWS USE A SYSTEM OF LEAP YEARS. SO AS THE CHRISTIAN WORLD CELEBRATES THE YEAR 2000 THE JEWISH CALENDAR WILL HAVE ALREADY ENTERED THE YEAR 5760.

HISTORY, MORALITY, AND SUFFERING

Judaism has a long history of persecution, not least because for over 1,500 years every Jew was personally charged by the Christian faith with responsibility for the death of Jesus Christ.

THE GUILT OF CRUCIFIXION

In the expanding Roman Empire of pagan times, the Jews endured the discrimination felt by other races and cults that had been swallowed up in the extending boundaries. Significantly, few Jews were ever given Roman citizenship which was, at the time, the ultimate symbol of belonging. However, by the time the Empire was Christianized in the 4th century, the fate of Judaism was sealed—it was considered that, as it was the Jews who had put Jesus on the cross, they should therefore suffer. In fact, it was only a small number of Jews with a vested interest in his demise who engineered Jesus's death. Most were willing listeners or even followers.

The conduct of those few Jews inspired the Crusaders of the Middle Ages to commit atrocities against any members of the Jewish population they happened upon en route to fight the Moors. For years it was standard for European Jews, a minority in any of the countries in which they settled, to wear identifying marks on their clothes, to be subjected to restrictive business practices, and even to live in one specified neighborhood—which soon turned into a ghetto.

THE DREYFUS AFFAIR

Gradually the Jews became integrated into Europe, finally receiving emancipation after the unification of the German empire in 1871. The Dreyfus affair in France at the turn of the 20th century revealed widespread anti-Semitism, and this helped to end it. An army officer, by the name of Albert Dreyfus, was accused of spying for Germany and was consequently jailed. Whispers that he was framed because he was Jewish soon became shouts, dividing the whole country. Many people, oblivious to the bad feeling against Jews, were horrified. Dreyfus was released and eventually cleared; for a while, anti-Semitism was laid to rest. However, the onset of World War II revived ancient anti-Semitic sentiments across Europe.

But these were emotions which had never been suppressed in Russia, where Jews were sometimes prevented from receiving even an education. Far worse, from 1881 onward, pogroms, or organized brutality against the Jews, were instituted. Some of the worst events occurred in 1906 as the government tried to deflect the dissatisfaction of workers by engendering hate against Judaism. About 600 cities, towns, and villages succumbed and as a result thousands died while their homes and businesses were looted and destroyed.

To help itself, the government sensationally revealed a worldwide conspiracy by the Jews in a book called *Protocols of the Elders of Zion*, first published in 1905. It was, of course, a vicious and deadly hoax, but the text was still being quoted after the 1917 revolutions in Russia when yet another pogrom took place.

GLOBAL ANTI-SEMITISM

The content of the same book was repeated in America in the newspaper *Dearborn Independent*, run by car magnate Henry Ford; he was widely condemned and later apologised.

Anti-Semitism in America sprang up because of the radical politics associated with Judaism, although the country has since become a haven for oppressed Jews. Measures against Jews by the Communists were also a matter of concern, but the situation has improved with the collapse of the Iron Curtain.

Above: Jews expelled from Russia in 1881. The authorities fostered a fear and loathing of the Jewish people throughout Russia to deflect attention from internal unrest sparked by mismanagement of the state.

Further relief for the hard-pressed Jewish population came from the Second Vatican Council (1962–1965), which formally repudiated the charge that all Jews were responsible for the death of Christ.

> **"Without screaming or weeping, these people undressed, stood around in family groups, kissed each other, said farewells and waited for the sign from the SS man who stood beside the pit with a whip in his hand."**

"During the 14 minutes I stood near, I heard no complaint or plea for mercy. I watched a family . . . an old woman with snow-white hair was holding a child of about one in her arms, singing to it and tickling it. The child was cooing with delight.

"The parents were looking on with tears in their eyes. The father was holding the hand of a boy about ten years old and speaking to him softly; the boy was fighting back the tears. The father pointed to the sky, stroked his head and seemed to explain something to him. At that

THE HOLOCAUST

moment the SS man at the pit started shouting something to his comrade. The comrade counted off about 20 people and instructed them to go behind the earth mound. Among them was the family . . .

"I looked at the man who did the shooting. He was an SS man who sat at the edge of the narrow end of the pit, his feet dangling into it. He had a tommy gun on his knees and was smoking a cigarette."

These were the words of Herman Graebe, a German civilian engineer who built roads in the Ukraine. He held the courtroom at Nuremburg in horrified silence as he related the work he saw carried out by Nazi death squads in Russia against the resident population of Jews.

A TERRIFYING DISCOVERY

Allied soldiers who were pushing Hitler's armies back into Germany in 1944 and 1945 saw at first hand the effects of the holocaust. They came across the death camps where charred limbs still protruded from the ovens which had killed untold thousands. The air was foul with the stench of death. Those left alive were bony, disease-ridden, and covered with sores and vermin. Only a few could be saved.

The holocaust was Hitler's Final Solution to the Jewish "question." Its legacy to later Jewish generations was one of enduring horror, paranoia, and frustration, and guilt on the part of those who survived.

Hitler came to power in 1933 and attacks on the minorities soon became commonplace, tolerated, and even encouraged by the government. In 1935 the Nuremberg Laws were passed which deprived German Jews of their citizenship. Abusive posters bearing such messages as "Let Judah perish" and "Jews not wanted here" mushroomed around the cities and Jews were compelled to wear clothes "branded" with the yellow Star of David. Some 250,000 Jews fled from Germany during the 1930s.

Few could have imagined the horrors that were still to come. In November 1938 came the *Kristallnacht* when the Nazis perpetrated a horrifying wave of violence against Jewish businesses, homes, synagogues, and, of course, the

Above: **Bodies of people reduced to skin and bone were awaiting cremation when the Allies liberated Buchenwald.**

and the result was the holocaust. From July 1941, measures against the Jews were stepped up. By 1942 news of the mass murders carried out in the extermination camps of Auschwitz, Treblinka, Wolzek, Buchenwald, and Belsen had reached the incredulous ears of Allied commanders. At this stage there was palpable disbelief that any nation was capable of such cruelty and consequently the activities of the Nazis were not included in Allied propaganda.

Nobody knows how many died in the Nazi death camps—the figure of six million is popularly quoted. Just as the Nazis were not all Germans—many were Latvians, Lithuanians, Ukrainians, Czechs, and others—not every concentration camp victim was a Jew. Hitler persecuted gypsies, Slavs, homosexuals, the physically and mentally handicapped, Communists, and anyone who opposed him. However, the Jews were in the majority. Bleak estimates are that one-third of European Jewry was wiped out by Hitler's "Final Solution."

Eminent members of the German High Command who survived the war were dealt with by the Allies in a war crimes trial at Nuremberg which opened on November 12, 1945. Justice Robert Jackson, the American attorney, said in his opening speech, "The wrongs which we seek to condemn and punish have been so calculated, so malignant, and so devastating, that civilization cannot tolerate their being ignored because it cannot survive their being repeated."

people themselves. Those that remained were, sooner or later, rounded up and sent to concentration camps. Life was hard, food was scarce, and illness and death common in the concentration camps. Even so, worse awaited them.

GENOCIDE

As the boundaries of the Reich extended during World War II, so the number of Jews under German control expanded. Nazis looked for ways to accelerate the death rate among Jews

Left: **Propaganda orchestrated by the Nazis, like this detail from a picture book published at Nuremburg in 1936, engendered public hostility toward the Jews.**

CHAPTER FOUR
HINDUISM

A faith of one God—or 330 million gods. To Western eyes Hinduism is a mass of contradictions. How else can one describe it when the sacred texts have a choice of different endings—none of which are considered wrong? There is no indisputable truth for Hindus, but many different aspects of the same truth.

This maze of mythology, mysticism, and free-flowing belief has evolved over thousands of years. The creed of the charioteering Aryans who overran India more than 3,000 years ago was then superimposed upon—and molded by—the indigenous religions of the country. Since then it has absorbed the influences of other faiths and cults like a sponge.

Short on dogma and doctrine, it is consequently unwieldy, eccentric, chaotic, and difficult to understand. For the student looking for a clear-cut definition, it just does not exist. Yet to millions of Indians this rambling umbrella of a religion brings comfort, color, and joy.

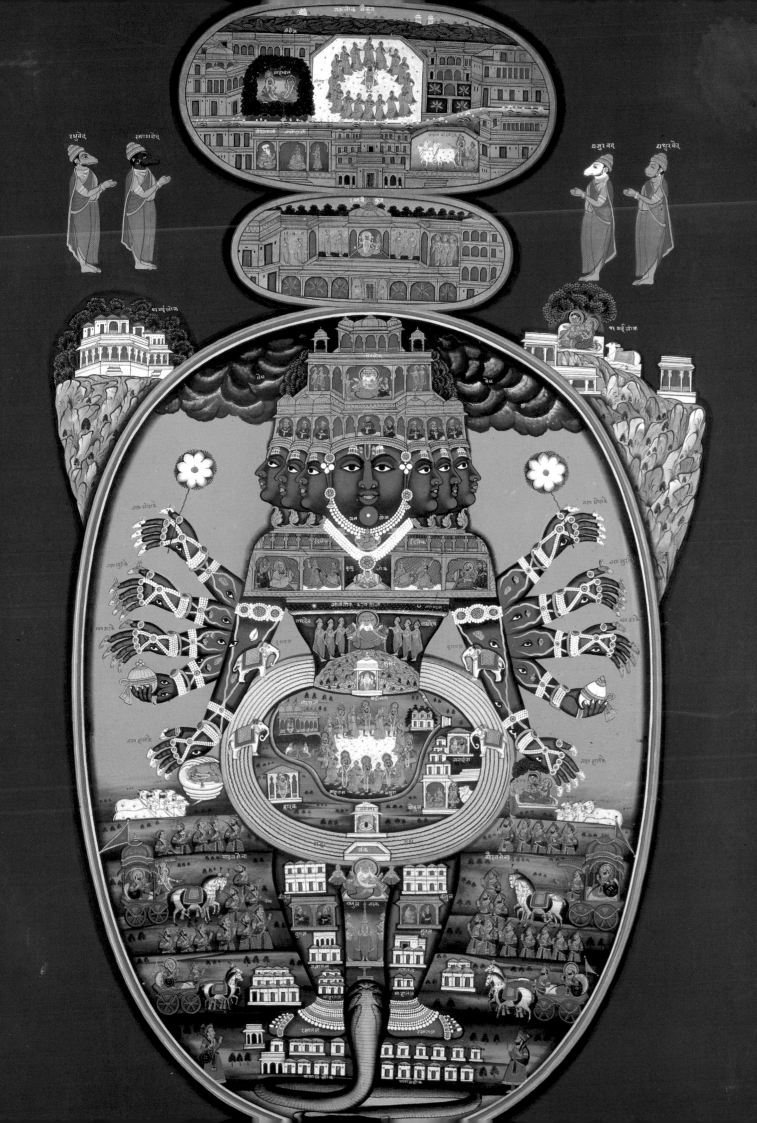

> "Verily, in the beginning this world was Brahman. It knew only itself: 'I am Brahman.' Therefore it became the All. Whoever of the gods became awakened to this, he indeed became it; likewise in the case of seers, likewise in the case of men. Whoever thus knows, 'I am Brahman' becomes this All." *Brihad-aranyaka Upanishad.*

ONE GOD – OR MANY?

Through the eyes of other faiths, Hinduism appears to be crowded with gods. Not so, according to the learned men of India.

The various gods featured in the Hindu faith are different manifestations of the same deity, the single spirit or the one Reality. For Hindus, God has many characteristics and numerous names and it is through this roundabout route, of offering worship to one god or many, that union with the true God is achieved. These minor gods are many voices singing the same song. A Christian or Islamic equivalent might be the saints acknowledged by both faiths, who are inspirational and powerful, yet rank below the all-powerful God.

THE GODS

The principal gods are Vishnu, Shiva, and Brahma, a holy trinity who themselves are all part of one god called Brahman. In outline Vishnu—wedded to Saraswati, the Goddess of Knowledge—is benevolent and his concern for the world brings him back down to earth as an *avatar*, or reincarnation. Vishnu has ten *avatars*, nine of which have already appeared. They are as follows:

The Fish (Matsya)—savior of Manu, the first man, after the great flood.

The Tortoise (Kuma)—the gods became immortal with his help.

The Boar (Varaha)—earth was rescued by him when it fell into a cosmic ocean.

The Man-Lion (Narasimha)—he killed a threatening demon.

The Dwarf (Vamana)—as a dwarf he is told by the evil King Bali he can have as much of the earth as he can cover in three strides. Vishnu changed shape and spanned the earth, air, and sky in just two.

Rama the Axe (Parashu Rama)—the warrior who protected the priests.

Rama, king of the Ayodhya—the Just King.

Krishna—a naughty child who grew to be an

Left: **Ganesh or Ganesa was beheaded by his father, Shiva, who then replaced the severed head with that of the first animal he found.**

Left: A scene from the *Ramayana* which, translated from Sanskrit, means "romance of Rama." An epic poem in seven books which centers on one man's struggle to save his abducted wife.

amorous cowherd and slayer of the evil Kamsa.

Buddha—the teacher.

Kalkin—still to come, the horseman who will bring an end to evil at the end of the age.

Shiva, otherwise known as Rudra, is a turbulent deity to be kept at arm's length—even when he is in the guise of Shambhu and Shankara, calmer aspects of the same god, he is awesome. The worship devoted to him is frequently through phallic representation.

His partner is Shakti, the Great Goddess, who also has different sides. As Kali she is terrible and bloodthirsty and her human devotees, known as "thugs," would murder to please her. Even today blood sacrifices to appease Kali are common. And as India enters the 21st century the hideous scandal of child sacrifice still bubbles just beneath the surface. Evidence that it occurs is being gathered together, while the vast majority of the population are horrified that India remains shackled to this dark aspect of its history. As Parvati Shakti, she is a beautiful bride. Her third character is as Durga and a cult devoted to her is prominent in Bengal.

Brahma is a god of little consequence, if there can be such a thing. His significance lies in his close parallel to the divinity.

The pursuit of enlightenment by Hindu men has traditionally been divided into four distinct phases. The first starts in childhood and involves tuition from a *guru*, lasting for a dozen years. After this chaste time he is expected to marry and begin a family. Twenty-five years later, when his children are grown, his destination is an *ashram*, or retreat for contemplation and teaching. Finally, in his old age, he renounces all material things in his life, takes to the road, and begs for food in an alms bowl. The sight of such men, called *sannyasins*, is still common in India. This life plan weds obligation to and renunciation from society in order that the cycle of life may continue.

YOGA AND YOGIS

Asceticism or self-discipline is a major factor in the life of a devout Hindu. Yoga also plays a crucial role. By tradition the system of yoga, pioneered by Pantanjali in the 2nd century B.C., touches on social morality, personal morality, posture, breath control, control of the senses, and concentration meditation to achieve union with God. Today the modern understanding of yoga, even in the East, is as a device to fine-tune physical postures and aid meditation.

Hindu yogis became famous for their mystic abilities, including clairvoyance, telepathy, mind-reading, levitation, and materialization. These powers are known as *siddhis*, Sanskrit for "perfect abilities."

OTHER HINDU GODS

AGNI	GOD OF FIRE
BRAHMA	GOD OF CREATION
BRAHMAN	THE ULTIMATE REALITY
GANESH	ELEPHANT-HEADED SON OF SHIVA
GANGA	PERSONIFICATION OF THE RIVER GANGES
HANUMAN	MONKEY GOD
MITRA	GOD OF LIGHT
PURUSHA	COSMIC MAN

SACRED TEXTS

India is a secular country—but one in which the dominant religion has a profound effect. Blissfully unaware of the contents of many of the sacred texts, Hindus have enormous freedom in choosing which path to follow. Horoscopes are more likely to influence the everyday choices of Hindus than the old scriptures.

Perhaps the biggest influence on their faith is exerted by the *gurus*, personal teachers who are less bothered with academia and more concerned with social and spiritual enlightenment. For centuries it was judged to be of greater value to hear words from the mouth of a guru and learn them by heart to repeat to the next generation, than to sit down and simply read a book.

THE UPANISHADS

Out of this tradition came the *Upanishads*. The very word is reminiscent of the gurus. It comprises *upa*, meaning near, *ni*, meaning down, and *shad*, meaning sitting. They are the collected wisdom of numerous gurus, gathered by their pupils or disciples and written in prose or verse in Sanskrit between 500 and 200 B.C. The aim is to link the student to God by first

"Those who do not know the field walk time and again over the treasure hidden beneath their feet and do not find it: in the same way all creatures pass through the world of Brahman day by day, but do not find it for they are carried away by unreality."

illustrating the relationship that exists between them. Sensitive tuition is the key, as the extract from the *Chandogya Upanishad* reveals.

The union between man and God is thoroughly explored. There is a famous story about a boy seeking the real truth about divinity from his father and being told, "You are yourself that very thing."

It is the *Upanishads* that consolidate the view that there is only one God. Their predecessor, the *Vedas*, oldest of the Hindu scriptures, leaves room for doubt. This was the literature handed down by the Aryan invaders who swarmed over India from the north in about 1750 B.C. In total there are four *Vedas*, the most eminent being the first, the "Rig Veda," or "Veda of Praise."

In it there are 1,017 hymns divided into ten sections, or *mandalas*, dedicated to the gods of the Aryans. Among the gods were Varuna, ruler of the heavens and seas, and Indra, the warrior. However, the finale is the "Song of Creation," which tantalizingly suggests that there is an all-powerful entity about which the gods knew nothing.

THE EPIC POEMS

Significant, too, are the epic poems *Mahabharata* and *Ramayana* which are in a collection of writings known as the *Puranas*. The *Mahabharata* is a breath-taking 100,000 couplets which examines the feud between the Pandavas and the Kauravas. Rich with allegory, this mammoth work contains the "Bhagavad Gita," the "Song of the Adorable One," perhaps the best-loved Hindu scripture. One of the Pandavas, Arjun, is filled with doubt before going into battle against the Kauravas who are, after all, his kinsmen. His charioteer is the god Krishna in disguise, who imparts his teachings, banishes Arjun's doubt, and expounds the necessity for devotion to God.

The *Ramayan* is shorter, dates from 500 years after the *Mahabharata*, and is believed to be the work of one man, Valmiki. Forced into exile, Prince Rama's wife Sita is kidnapped by a demon and held captive on the island of Sri Lanka. Rama and his brother Lakshman search for her and finally rescue her after she is located by Hanuman, king of the monkeys. It is a story of valor, fidelity, and perseverance in which good triumphs over evil.

THE LAWS OF MANU

From a similar era to the *Ramayana* come the *Laws of Manu*, in which are set the comprehensive rules for spiritual, moral, ethical, and civil dilemmas. It was the wisdom of the gods imparted to Manu that established the caste system and condemned countless thousands of people to misery over the ensuing centuries.

Hindus believe that some of the writings revered in their faith are *sruti*, revelations of God. Others are *smrti*, remembered texts which are not as highly regarded.

"Let there be good to all, let all be free from sickness, let us all see good and, let none suffer." Part of a Vedic Prayer.

Concern about death and the afterlife is probably what drives most people into the arms of a faith. For Hindus the journey to unity with God is longer than most.

THE KARMIC WHEEL

Hindus believe in reincarnation. That means the soul is reborn into another body after death to endure a further life. This is not a matter to rejoice over for the aim is to leave the wheel of rebirth—*samsara*, as it is known in Sanskrit—to be reunited with Brahman, the Absolute.

REINCARNATION

The law of cause and effect governing reincarnation is called *karma* which translates from Sanskrit to "deed." In essence every physical action, word, and thought is accounted for, not in this life but in the next. Goodliness will be rewarded, while punishments await those who have erred. It is a chain which

cannot be broken, but will hopefully come to a natural end if a person follows the three "Pure Precepts:" cease evil, do good for others, and keep a pure mind.

In Biblical terms it adds up to the old adage of reaping what you sow but, of course, in Christian philosophy the results are seen at the day of reckoning, rather than in a new life or cycle of new lives.

With reincarnation as a central theme, Hinduism once again provides more than just a faith; it is also a code for everyday living which encourages good conduct. Those people who are particularly evil may return to earth in the guise of an animal or another lower life form.

Agami-karma refers to present causes and effects, *prarabdha-karma* is already caused and is in the process of being effected, and *sanchita-karma* is similarly already caused, but has yet to take effect.

The belief in reincarnation dates back to the *Vedas* and is reinforced in the *Upanishads*. Like the caste system, it has been used by priests as a stick to keep the lower orders in their place.

There's no scientific proof to back up theories on reincarnation, but the anecdotal evidence is intriguing. Almost always it comes from the mouths of very young children.

SHANTI DEVA

Consider the case of little Shanti Deva. In 1935 she told her parents of a place called Muttra where she had once lived. Her name, she said, was Ludgi and she was a mother of three who died in childbirth. Her family were reluctant to believe her—until they discovered there was indeed a place called Muttra where a woman, Ludgi, had died in labor. When Shanti visited Muttra with her family for the first time she

Left: **The rebirth of Brahma for the new creation. Brahma was born from the navel of Vishnu from which a lotus flower grew; within it was the three-headed god. Vishnu reclines upon a serpent floating on primeval waters.**

IN HINDUISM, GOD IS OFTEN REPRESENTED BY THE SOUND OF OM OR AUM. THE A STANDS FOR THE POWER OF GOD THE CREATOR, THE U IS FOR GOD THE PRESERVER, AND THE M FOR GOD AND THE POWER TO DESTROY. HINDUS MEDITATE TO THE SOUND OF AUM.

lapsed into the local dialect and recognized her (former) husband and two older children.

Investigators have identified four areas where there might be similarities between living people and personas from the past.

"A man is the creator of his own fate, and even in his fetal life he is affected by the dynamics of the works of his prior existence . . ."
The Garuda Purana

Those claiming to be reincarnations of others might be able to recall names, dates, and personal facts; they might recognize places and people who are otherwise unknown to them; they sometimes behave like the person they claim they once were; and finally they might look similar or bear certain mirror-image marks. Sometimes birthmarks have been associated with death wounds from a previous existence, too.

India is famous for its caste system, ancient divisions of society into which people are born and may never leave. The Hindu caste system—or *varna* as it is known in Sanskrit—began with four main divisions. Brahmans are the priests, Ksatriyas the warriors, Vaisyas the merchants, and Sudras the servants. According to mythology the castes came from Purusha, the father-figure of humankind.

POSITIONS IN LIFE

—The *Brahmans* came from his mouth—the highest part.
—The powerful *Ksatriyas* were from his arms.
—The *Vaisyas* were born of his thighs.
—The *Sudras*, the laborers, from the lowest part, his feet.

Only boys from the first three castes were permitted to undergo the sacred thread ceremony in which they crossed the threshold from childhood to adulthood. Seated around a fire, boy and Brahmin priest chanted prayers and hymns. Afterward a red thread was symbolically wound around the shoulders and waist of the initiate, who became known as "twice-born" and the duty of prayer was upon him.

More castes emerged over time to account for new branches of Indian society and there were classes within each one. In the census of 1901 there were 2,378 castes identified and several hundred sub-castes. Those outside the caste system were considered impure and branded the Untouchables. At the bottom of the pile, they were given only the lowliest jobs.

PUNISHMENT BY REBIRTH

The threat of reincarnation as an Untouchable was present in the *Chandogya Upanishad* and it was an effective one. "Those who are of good conduct here—the prospect is that they will come to a pleasant birth, either the birth of a priest, or the birth of a warrior, or the birth of a merchant. But those who are of evil conduct here—the prospect is that they will come to an evil birth, either the birth of a dog, or the birth of a swine, or the birth of an outcast."

"Mixed" marriages were not allowed. It was impossible to escape the confines of the caste system. Segregation was scrapped, at least officially, largely through the efforts of one man.

Right: **Gandhi knew the benefits of peaceful protest. During this demonstration in 1925 he devoted his time to spinning instead of shouting.**

"GREAT SOUL"

Mohandas Gandhi (1869–1948) was born in India, but studied law in England and was called to the bar in Bombay, before moving to South Africa to improve the lives of his fellow Indians who had migrated there. It was here that he learned the value of peaceful protest.

In 1914 he returned to India determined to expel the British colonials. Already the reputation of this short, slight, bespectacled man was colossal. He became leader of the Indian National Congress, the political party formed to fight for independence. Gandhi's watchword was *satyagraha*, a Sanskrit expression for non-violent resistance.

In tandem with his patient campaign for Indian home rule—which earned him a prison sentence from anxious British rulers in 1922—Gandhi's other chief concern was for the Untouchables. Appalled at their plight, Gandhi forced Indians to rethink their attitudes which kept the unfortunate caste-less elements of society in grinding poverty. He renamed the Untouchables the *Harijan*, or Children of God, and denounced the caste system which consigned them to the trash heap of society, saying, "There is nothing so bad in the world."

In 1932 he forced some changes on the issue by undertaking his first "fast unto death." Unwilling to martyr this determined man with a mighty following, authorities made partial concessions to help the Untouchables.

A leading participant in the independence talks that followed the World War II, Gandhi advocated that Hindus and Muslims should live peacefully, side by side. It was this stance, which was fatally misconstrued as support for the Muslim minority, that cost him his life. Fearing Hinduism would be overwhelmed by Islam, the fanatical Nathuram Godse fought his way to the front of the crowd that thronged around Gandhi on Friday, January 30, 1948, as he made his way to evening prayers. Godse drew a revolver from his shirt and fired four times. Three of the bullets found their target and the 78-year-old Gandhi died within 30 minutes. Although he never held office, Gandhi was considered the founder of modern India and was known by the name Mahatma, or "Great Soul."

Thanks to the efforts of Gandhi, the caste system was abolished in India in 1948 and discrimination was outlawed. Nevertheless, after years of conditioning, it remains impossible to eradicate prejudice in Hindu society.

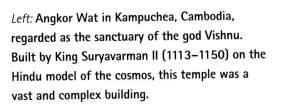

Left: **Angkor Wat in Kampuchea, Cambodia, regarded as the sanctuary of the god Vishnu. Built by King Suryavarman II (1113–1150) on the Hindu model of the cosmos, this temple was a vast and complex building.**

TEMPLES

Hindus have the option of prayer, or *puja*, anywhere and everywhere. For them the universe is a temple of worship and most homes have a shrine in which *puja* is usually performed three times daily. Yet it is renowned for its exotic temples, bedecked with flowers and fragrant with the smell of incense. To those accustomed to the idiosyncratic nature of Hinduism, it will come as no surprise to learn that many visit the temples and pay homage to the Deity, but may not remain to pray.

India's finest temples, some of which are ancient, are to be found in the south. Many in the north were destroyed by Muslims offended by the apparent idolatry of the Hindus.

WITHIN THE TEMPLE

Temples vary in terms of their age and shape but usually they share some common features. Generally, the door faces the rising sun. On the ground in front of the temple there is frequently a statue which acts as a temple guardian. When the temple is dedicated to Shiva, the guardian is the bull Nandi, Vishnu has the bird Garuda, and Durga a fierce lion.

Inside there is the *mandapa*, a grand pillared hall, beyond which lies the shrine. The object in the shrine represents the Deity and it is covered by a canopy, parasol, or pyramid roof. Worship is directed less at the idol than at the spirit behind it and this will continue until God's face is known. Hindu teaching decrees: "One needs images and symbols so long as God is not realized in his true form. It is God himself who has provided these various forms of worship to suit different stages of spiritual growth."

There is a priest in attendance who is responsible for making the offering brought by visitors and, in turn, rewarding them with *prasad*, a gift from the god which is generally dried fruit, nuts, and sugar crystals.

THE FIVE MAIN PRINCIPLES OF HINDUISM MAY BE SUMMED UP AS PARMESHWAR (GOD), PRARTHANA (PRAYER), PUNARJANMA (REBIRTH), PURUSHARTHA (LAW OF ACTION), AND PRANI DAYA (COMPASSION FOR LIVING THINGS).

Other images often found in Hindu temples are those of the revered Mohandas Gandhi, the Sikh founder Guru Nanak, and even Jesus, who is honored as a great teacher of God's message.

WORSHIP AROUND THE GLOBE

Outside India, Hindu temples have become a focus for the community, while congregational prayer, assuming a greater importance, has become more organized.

Although there are no set times for worship, Hindus will happily adapt to the country in which they live, and therefore Hindus living in Britain or America will have a Sunday morning service as that is when most enjoy a day away from work.

The worship is centered on the sacred fire, sparked in a portable fire altar containing wood and clarified butter, or *ghee*. Only the priest can initiate the offering of fire, or *havan*.

Before putting himself before God, the worshipper must be pure. To achieve this he undertakes a ritual of daubing his ears, nose, eyes, mouth, arms, body, and legs with water. The priest recites from the *Vedas* and also says prayers to the chief gods.

Then comes the ceremonial offering of love and devotion, or *arti*, which is open to everyone. A tray with five lights upon it is waved in front of the Deity and flowers, incense, water, and ether may be presented to the statues. All the foreheads in the Temple, whether they be human or image, are dotted with red paste before the congregation donates money and receives God's blessing by placing their hands over the flames and rubbing the heat into his forehead and hair.

There are hymns accompanied by tambourines, drums, and communal clapping. Dancing is another form of Hindu devotion and, with the rise in popularity of ethnic dancing in the West, one of the most easily accessible to the Westerner.

"From the unreal lead me to the real. From the darkness lead me to light. From death lead me to immortality."
Upanishads

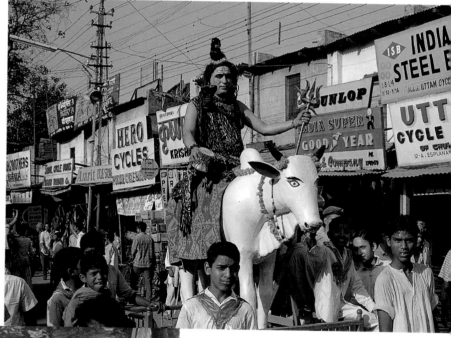

Above: In India the white cow is considered especially sacred to Hindus and its meat is never eaten. Consequently, it often appears during religious parades.

Left: The worship of fire among Hindus is widespread. By rubbing the heat from sacred flames over their bodies the faithful are conveying the blessing of God.

CELEBRATIONS

A riot of color, a cacophony of noise, Hindu festivals are a thorough assault on the senses. One of the best loved is *Divali* or *Diwali*, a four-day New Year festival, but because the Hindu calendar differs from the Gregorian calendar, the celebration is usually held in October or November. Shared with the Sikhs, *Diwali* translates to a "festival of light." It is held during the last two days of an old moon and the advent of a new moon. Houses, streets, temples, and barns are festooned with lights, either electric or oil-fueled.

THE FESTIVAL OF LIGHT

At New Year the emphasis is on renewal, so there are new clothes for everyone—the rich providing garments for the poor. Houses are whitewashed and cleaned, and even pets and livestock are spruced up. Gifts are exchanged, too, so Hindus who have moved away from India to Western countries often describe the season as "our Christmas."

In typically Hindu fashion the tale behind the festival varies tremendously. Some believe it is significant as the birth of the goddess Kali. Another story says that Lakshmi, the female partner of Vishnu, visits houses bearing the gift of prosperity, favoring the cleanest and brightest houses. A further tale maintains that *Diwali* marks the victory by Krishna over the demon Naraka of Assam. Legend has it that the vanquished Naraka made one final request of Krishna. "On the anniversary of my death

everyone should be happy, wear new clothes, let off fireworks, burn lights to brighten the night, and send one another greetings." Yet another famous triumph, that of Vishnu over King Bali, is also given as the reason for celebrating *Diwali*.

Perhaps the most widely accepted explanation is in the story of the *Ramayana*, that the festival marks the return of Rama as the rightful heir to the throne. Giant effigies of Ravanna, the demon king and enemy of Rama, are burnt at *Diwali*.

THE FIREWALKER

In spring there is a festival called *Holi*. Although it probably had its roots in an ancient fertility ritual, there is a captivating myth explaining its origins. A king by the name of Hiranyakapishu was so vain that he demanded all his subjects should worship only him. Most of them did, but his young son, Prahlada, refused. This boy was devoted to Hinduism, so much so that he would chant the names of the gods. His father was so infuriated that he wished his son dead. He called on his daughter Holika who possessed magic powers and was able to walk through fire without being burned. At her father's bidding, Holika picked up her brother and walked through a furnace. Little did she know that her powers were diminished when she entered the flames with someone else. So Holika died while Prahlada, who spent his time reciting the names of the gods, emerged unscathed.

There are many more Hindu festivals, not least the annual procession from each and every temple, led by the temple image which is carried by the worshippers. There are also well-defined daily observances in Hinduism.

THE GANGES

The ritual of morning bathing is important to Hindus, as it leaves the body refreshed and ready for prayer. Just as important is the purification of the inner self. One way of achieving this, according to the *Brahmandapurana*, is to take a dip in the Ganges, the river that winds through India. So sacred is the Ganges that one Hindu prayer comprises 108 different names of the river. Mythology has it that the Ganges was once the constellation of stars known as the Milky Way.

According to Hindu lore: "Those who bathe devoutly once in the pure currents of the Ganga, their tribes are protected by Her from hundreds of thousands of dangers. Evils accumulated through generations are destroyed. Just by bathing in the Ganga one gets immediately purified."

Not all Hindu traditions have found a place in the 20th century. One of the most notorious was *suttee*, a practice in which Indian widows sacrificed themselves on their husband's funeral pyre. By doing so, a widow was thought to ensure salvation for both. Thanks to the campaigning of Rammohun Roy (1772–1833) the convention was outlawed.

The temple at Jaganatha was also the scene of horrible excesses. A mighty cart was ritually pulled through the town and the faithful would throw themselves to their deaths under the wheels. The cart was so enormous it gave the word "juggernaut" to the English language.

Above left: **Spring is marked by the festival of *Holi* which has its roots in fertility rituals. A pail of brightly colored paint is about to be thrown over revelers as part of the celebrations.**

Right: **The power and spirituality of the River Ganges is a major phenomenon in India. People, like these women at Benares, believe that praying and bathing in it will protect them from evil.**

CHAPTER FIVE
EASTERN RELIGIONS

The modern age of materialism in the West has inspired many disillusioned city-dwellers to look to the ancient religions of the East for spiritual satisfaction. India and China were vast rural lands with a people who were characteristically more attuned to religion than to the secular lifestyle that pervaded Western ways. For the Westerner these are the natural homes of the alternative faiths.

There are two complementary principles in Chinese religion: yin and yang. One is passive, one active, and they are perpetually fluid. A piece of each resides in the other and, to achieve harmony, a balance must be made.

In India the Hindus have long been tolerant of other faiths (with the exception of Muslims) and for this reason many sects have flourished there, frequently adopting aspects of the host religion. One common facet of Indian religion is asceticism, self-denial for spiritual enhancement, probably inspired by the dominant Hindu faith.

TAO

To understand Tao is to climb inside the head of an Oriental person and see things from a different perspective.

Tao—pronounced *dow*—is passive rather than active, spontaneous not structured, but fatalist and freely flowing. It is the principle of all things. The Constituents of Tao are peace, meditation, naturalness, serenity—otherwise known as the philosophies of Quietists. Although no action is advocated, nothing is left undone. This persistent state of inaction is known as *wu-wei*.

Tao is wary of the values we insert into life rather than those that occur naturally—for example, good and evil, health and sickness. These are, according to Taoists, just the surface elements rather than the fundamentals.

It is also a fascinating paradox for "the way" cannot be followed or taught even though Tao controls the universe and all within it. Man's goal is to unite himself with Tao.

THE HIDDEN SAGE

The father of Taoism is Lao Tzu, a figure so shrouded in mystery that he has earned himself the title of "hidden sage." He is said to have lived in the 6th century B.C., although some insist he never lived at all. Those who believe he walked the earth claim he was an archivist and astrologer in the Emperor's administration and was visited by Confucius.

The pair did not see eye to eye and the philosophies each spawned continue to be at odds.

As the dynasty which he served fell into decline, Lao Tzu embarked on a trip to the wild westerly provinces of China. A guard at a frontier-post lamented the departure of the wise and learned sage and asked him to write down his teachings, resulting in the *Tao-Te-Ching*. Once the work had been completed Lao Tzu disappeared into the mountains, never to be seen again. He was estimated to be about 180 years old.

The *Tao-Te-Ching*, which translates to "The Book of the Way and of Virtue," comprises two books of 37 and 44 chapters. However, the authorship of the *Tao-Te-Ching* remains in doubt as it appears to date from far later than the life of Lao Tzu.

Other canonical material pertaining to Tao was produced by, and is named after, Chuang Tzu (350–275 B.C.) and is generally considered to be more accessible than that of Lao Tzu.

After the philosophy of Tao came the religion of the same name. In the 2nd century, Lao Tzu was deified, and the theory of Tao became transformed into a religion, Taoism. Its instigator was Chang Tao-Ling who revealed a succession of "Celestial Masters" at the head

"Once Chuang Chou dreamt he was a butterfly, a butterfly flitting and fluttering about, happy with himself, and doing as he pleased. He didn't know he was Chuang Chou. Suddenly he woke up and there he was, solid and unmistakably Chuang Chou. But he didn't know if he was Chuang Chou who dreamt he was a butterfly, or a butterfly dreaming he was Chuang Chou."

of Taoism. As a religion it had two faces, one of popular worship and the second which was infused with mysticism and closely linked to Shamanism. (See page 18.)

THE PURSUIT OF HARMONY

Adepts take tremendous spiritual journeys to a place with a vantage point from which they can see the world in harmony or as one. The subject of alchemical study, it openly discusses the elixir of life and its benefits. According to Chuang Tzu, "Life and death are one, right and wrong are the same." These are alien notions to those with no feel for the Chinese Way. Tao is difficult to appreciate fully for those Westerners who have a tendency to pigeon-hole ideas. Perhaps Tao is best understood in the words of the Chinese masters:

"The Way is like an empty vessel
That yet may be drawn from
Without ever needing to be filled.
It is bottomless; the very progenitor
of all things in the world.
In it all sharpness is blunted,
All tangles untied,
All glare tempered,
All dust smoothed.
It is like a deep pool that never dries."

"(There was) something
mysteriously formed,
Born before heaven and earth . . .
Perhaps it is the mother of ten
thousand things.
I do not know its name.
Call it Tao."

Left: **Lao Tzu and Confucius, the giants of Chinese philosophy, allegedly met but never got along. Both schools of thought remain radically different.**

Probably the most famous Chinaman ever to have lived, Confucius (551–479 B.C.) bequeathed the world some admirable and enigmatic wisdom packaged in a series of books. Yet his theories were controversial and, during its vivid history, China would see great swings both for and against Confucianism.

CONFUCIUS

Below: A 17th century portrait of Confucius, reputedly the author of several major works although only one, the *Analects*, is likely to be his.

"All 300 odes in the *Classic of Poetry* can be summed up in one of its lines, 'Have no wrong thoughts'."
Analects

THE HUMBLE SAGE

Confucius was born in Shantung province in northern China at a time when the ancient Chinese civilization was becoming increasingly sophisticated. He was named K'ung Fu Tze, but this was later anglicized by Jesuit missionaries who lobbied the Pope to have the Chinese scholar canonized. Little is known of his parents although his father's name may have been Shu He. It is believed he was orphaned as a child by the death of his father and that he grew up in poverty. At least, that is what he maintained in later years by saying, "When young I was without rank and in humble circumstances." Historians have since pondered whether in fact he came from a noble family, as the education he received was clearly a privileged one. Yet it was his insight into the plight of the common people that made his principles so enduring. It is tempting to believe he learned this through his own experiences.

He married, had two children, and was left a widower at a young age, but little more is known about his personal life. "Those who can, do, and those who can't, teach" is an old English saying which seems applicable to Confucius. He aspired to a position in the courts of the ruling emperors but failed, so he became a teacher. By all accounts his lessons were more discussion group than lecture. His messages were firmly rooted in morals and ethics rather than faith, although he felt God

> "Men's natures are alike; it is their habits that carry them far apart." *Analects*

played a part in the teachings. "Heaven begat the good that is in me," he often said.

Despite a question mark over his tolerance levels, Confucius appears to have commanded respect and affection from his students. Indeed, it was through ex-pupils that he finally won a place on the Council of the State of Lu.

THE PROLIFIC TEACHER

At the age of 60 he threw up his comfortable lifestyle and traveled in search of a role as a high-ranking adviser to royalty, but once again was frustrated. He continued to teach and devote more time to writing. Yet he was not bitter—"I do not murmur against Heaven. I do not grumble against man. I pursue my studies here on earth and am in touch with Heaven above. It is Heaven that knows me."

At the time of his death he was the Master K'ung and "teacher of ten thousand generations" among his disciples, although it took some years for his fame to spread nationally.

His works were editions of the Five Classics: the *I Ching*, or Classic of Changes; the *Shu Ching*, or Classic of History; the *Shi Ching*; or Classic of Odes; the *Li Ching*, or Classic of Rights, and the *Chu'un Ch'iu*, or Spring and Fall Annals. The *Yueh Ching*, or Classic of Music, has been lost. Confucius has been credited with authorship of all the Classics, although they almost certainly include the work of others and may both post- and predate him.

In addition, the *Analects*, or Selected Sayings, contain the perceptive observations which gave Confucius his staying power and three other books—*The Great Learning*, the *Doctrine of Mean*, and the *Book of Mencius*—are vehicles for Confucian thought.

Above: **The colorful celebrations for Confucius's birthday which is still celebrated as one of the major festivals of the Chinese calendar. This Confucian temple is at T'aipie in northern Taiwan.**

Left: **An 18th-century scene depicting the life of Confucius and his disciples, with the Master giving advice to the faithful. He insisted man was born good and should always follow his true nature.**

Appalled at wholesale corruption in the state and the tyranny of the petty rulers, Confucius revived an old-style code of conduct to put matters right.

IN SEARCH OF YESTERYEAR

His inspiration was the China of his ancestors some 500 years previously, before the quareling feudal leaders governed—halcyon days of benevolence and harmony which benefited both the rulers and the ruled. Consequently, Confucius became the bizarre contradiction of a progressive reformer who looked backward instead of forward to achieve his aims.

Years before its arrival in distant Britain, Confucius sought to introduce an age of chivalry to China. His teachings attempted to engender a gentlemanly conduct between one and all which would set out the guidelines for life. He instructed that there were five relationships that should be accorded mutual respect: those of ruler and subject, father and son, older and younger brother, husband and wife, and friend and friend.

For such relationships to work there were two principles which Confucius held dear, known as *Li* and *Jen*. *Li* broadly translates to propriety, morals, manners, and respect of the ceremonial. *Jen* is seen as love of humanity, benign charity, and consideration to others.

IMPACT OF CONFUCIUS ON CHINA

SUPERIOR MAN

Through a combination of *li* and *jen* and taking the "Golden Mean," or the "Middle Way," there would emerge "Superior Man." Thereafter Confucius saw the orders of society harmonizing to everyone's advantage. He perceived little benefit in worship of the gods if the treatment of our fellow human beings fell by the wayside. Accordingly he respected heaven, or T'ien, and other spiritual matters, but

Left: **For years children were taught the wisdom of the sage Confucius and Chinese culture became a reflection of Confucian thought.**

CONFUCIUS'S LEGACY

Schools of Confucianism arose after his death, established by his numerous disciples. The most famous of his adherents were Mencius (390–305 B.C.) and Hsun Tzu (312–238 B.C.).

Mencius, like Confucius, attempted to pass on the wisdom of ages without imprinting his own message and character upon it. He emphasized the responsibility of society toward the poor, linking economics closely to ethics. The advantage of the system of *jen* for princes and emperors was the wealth of his state, the continuation of his line, and the loyalty of the people. Hsun Tzu advocated education and moral training, highlighting the value of study.

The popularity of Confucianism grew and grew. A grasp of Confucian thought became the measurement of success in the civil service exams in China. Probably because of this, the theories became imperceptibly intertwined with the Chinese way of life.

Confucianism graduated to cult status, with every town and city proudly building its temple dedicated to The Master until the religion declined after 1911 following the end of the dynastic reigns. Criticism leveled at this philosophical religion was that, like the Hindu caste system, it condemned people to their place in life and was often used to subjugate women.

"If you control the people by government acts and keep them in line with law and order, they will refrain from doing wrong, but they will not have a sense of honor or shame. But if you lead them through virtue and regulate them by the laws of propriety, then they will have a sense of shame and will attain goodness." *Analects*

did not center his philosophies upon them. Confucius believed the answer to humankind's essential dilemma was in proper government and guidance of human nature. However, there was one element of religion that particularly appealed to him—ancestral obligation.

The phrase much quoted in Confucian study is *hsiao*, or filial piety and is concerned with the issue of duty and devotion. Confucius himself was so absorbed in the responsibilities of the son that when his mother died, he gave up work and spent 27 months in mourning. The veneration of ancestors had long been a feature of Chinese religion and was actively endorsed by Confucianism.

Right: The Disciples of Confucius were often young men whose ambition was to become civil servants, like this tax collector pictured in 1690.

More than a religion, Shinto is a way of life for the Japanese. Its rituals, rites, and superstitions have passed from generation to generation and are now deeply ingrained. Today the observance of Shinto is low-key, yet it remains central to the existence of modern Japanese life.

SHINTO

Although an entirely Japanese religion, Shinto is derived from two Chinese words, *Shen*, meaning gods, and *Tao*, meaning way. Its history has long been fogged by the mists of time, but it probably evolved within the communities of Japan which themselves developed after invasion from the north and emigration from the east. There is no venerated founder or holy scriptures, but the religion nevertheless remains absolute.

KAMI

The focus of worship is the *kami*, a word that is often translated as "gods." In fact, it means much more. *Kami* is a concept rather than a word and refers to spirits, the elements, animals, crops, or anything that can be construed as divine. According to Motoori Norinaga, a student of Shinto, "All . . . things whatsoever which deserve to be dreaded and revered for the extraordinary and pre-eminent powers which they possess are called *kami*." It is popularly thought that there are around eight million *kami*.

Highest-ranking *kami* of all is Amaterasu Omigami, the "heaven-shining-august-goddess" who protects the Japanese. In Shinto mythology it is her grandchild Ninigi who descends to earth, and his great-grandson Jimmu who becomes the first Emperor of a unified Japan. Thereafter the Emperors of Japan assumed god-like qualities.

RITES AND FESTIVALS

Strong emphasis is placed on purity. The bereaved perform a series of rites to cleanse the dead and usher in peace and benevolence. Agricultural rites are also important, derived from an age when the Japanese lived—or died—by the success of their crops.

Principal among the Shinto festivals is the Kanname-sai in October. It involves the offering of the first of the rice crop to the Emperor, who duly savors it in the ceremony of Niiname-sai. There is also Hina Matsuri, a doll's festival for girls on March 3, while boys duly celebrate Koi-nobori with a display of streamers on posts.

"If you want to know, come unto me and I will explain to you the origin of all things. I, God the Parent, reveal myself and I will explain everything to you in detail; the whole world will rejoice. I hasten to save the world, therefore you people in the world exult." Shinto song.

Worship is offered to a *shintai*, a representation of the relevant *kami*.

The earliest records of Shinto date back to A.D. 712, although the *Kojiki*, the Record of Ancient Things, is in fact written in Chinese. Further tales were written in the *Nihongi*, an account of creation, while the ritual prayers gathered and published in A.D. 927 are known as *Engishiki*.

A MALLEABLE RELIGION

Shinto has known highs and lows in its popularity and has adapted to survive. With the influx of Buddhism from India via China there was a convergence of beliefs, so much so that even as early as the 6th century, it became difficult to distinguish Shinto from Buddhism. Another influence that helped to mold Shinto was that of Confucianism, again from China, and there were other smaller religions which put down roots in Japan. For centuries the faiths flourished side by side until a backlash in Japan against the imported philosophies during the 18th and 19th centuries brought about the emergence of the state of Shinto in 1890.

Already the country's religions had been divided into three distinct classes: Shinto, Buddhist, and Christian. Those outside of these were called Shinto sects, of which there were 13.

Shinto became known for its fervent nationalism and an accompanying belief that the Japanese were a superior race. It was this attitude, fostered over a number of years, that led to the Japanese offensive during World War II. The strength of faith that many Japanese had in their Emperor, Hirohito, was demonstrated by the actions of the kamikaze pilots, suicide bombers, who chose to die for his benefit.

Although the role of the Emperor has been much diminished in the past 50 years, nationalism and loyalty are still important in the daily lives of the Japanese.

Above: Iazanagi and Izanami are the creator deities in Japanese mythology. Their offspring included the sun goddess Amaterasu, supreme among the *kami*.

Below: Shinto priesthoods are hereditary. Their influence has, however, diminished since World War II after which Shinto was de-established as the state religion.

Shinto shrines are traditionally wooden and therefore no ancient ones remain. They are entered by one or more *torii*, or gateways. The pathway may be lined with lanterns donated by worshippers and there may be a dog, lion, or fox statue guarding the shrine. There is always a sacred sakaki tree in the vicinity.

To a Jain, all life is sacred. And Jains are not only concerned about the fate of fellow human beings —to kill the humblest fly is unacceptable, so to insure that insects are not accidentally swallowed, they wear a mask over their mouths and their drinking water is strained. Likewise, the most observant Jains will sweep the ground with a brush—traditionally with peacock feathers— before walking to clear any insect from their path. Even then they tread carefully. The most devout Jain will even avoid washing his body to keep the parasites living upon it safe from harm. The term for this non-violence is *ahimsa*.

JAINISM

It was the Jains' fundamental desire to preserve life that has led to the spread of vegetarianism throughout India. Their authority was such that this minority religion set the tenor for the rest of the country. As their beliefs precluded them from working in farming, the Jains made their living as merchants and many became extremely prosperous.

Today there are only a few million Jains left in existence in India as the religion has suffered a decline. This is probably due to the fact that it is not a missionary religion like its chief rival, Buddhism.

THE PROPHETS OF JAINISM

Jain is taken from the word *jina*, which means "victor." This was the title given to Jain teachers who sought to win the battle against bodily desires. Jainism was pioneered by the teacher Parsva in the 9th century B.C. as a reaction to the dominance of the Hindu Brahmin caste.

However, it is Mahavira (599–527 B.C.) who is remembered for establishing the Jains as a religious force. Mahavira, like the Buddha, came from the warrior caste. He was born near Patna to a local ruler and legend has it that, before his birth, his princess mother dreamt she would have a prophet for a son. His parents were already devotees of the Jain religion and, after his birth, they were determined to bring no further evil to the world so they fasted to death.

Mahavira married and had a family, but by the age of 30 embarked on an ascetic life. His lifestyle was so severe that he even abandoned his clothes, the last vestiges of his worldly goods. For 13 years he wandered India, begging for food and contemplating life's

"Non-violence is the highest religion" reads the inscription found in numerous Jain temples.

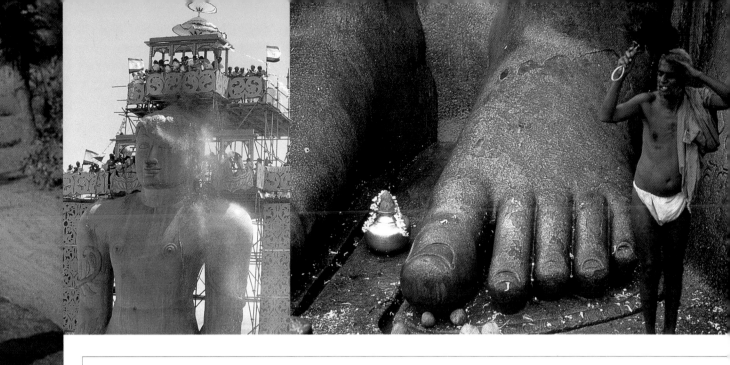

Left: A Jain pilgrim clad in white wears a mask and wields a broom to prevent the accidental slaughter of insects in his path.

Above left: A 54 ft statue of Lord Bahubali who the Digambara sect of Jainism believe was the first to achieve spiritual liberation.

Above right: Jains are split into different sects and have at least two versions of the holy scriptures. The Digambara believe in the abandonment of clothes for male devotees.

truths. He saw "all conditions of the world, of gods, men, and demons—all living things, where they come from and where they go to."

Gathering a band of disciples around him, Mahavira—the name means "great man"—began teaching and an order of monks was established. Mahavira was seen as the 24th Tirthamkara or "ford-maker," who crosses to the shore of realization. The first Tirthamkara lived millions of years ago; Parsva was the 23rd.

JAINIST WORSHIP

Monks and nuns are central to the continuing existence of Jainism. Divided into two orders, the Digambaras are "sky-clad," or naked in the same manner as their hero Mahavira. The

Svetambaras are "white-clad" and permitted three pieces of white cloth as garments. Monks observe five vows of non-violence, truthfulness, not stealing, denial of material goods, and chastity. The "three jewels" of the religion are right faith, right knowledge, and right conduct.

The Jain scriptures are known as the 11 Angas, or limbs. Once again we find that the religious theories were passed on by word of mouth for centuries before being written down. Although the details vary between Jain sects, the belief is that there are countless souls in the universe seeking entry to Nirvana. The souls are burdened with *karma*, the consequences of their actions, and only those who ascend the chain of life by accumulating good *karma* can hope for a heavenly afterlife.

There is no single God or pantheon of gods to worship, although Jain saints are venerated. The asceticism practiced by the Jains is awesome and rigid. Their austerity is known as *tapas*. Distressing though it may be to Westerners, the noblest ideal for a Jain saint is to starve himself to death.

TODAY THE SWASTIKA IS A CHILLING REMINDER OF THE NAZI REGIME OF HITLER'S GERMANY. IN FACT, HE PURLOINED THE SYMBOL FROM THE JAINS WHO USED IT AS THEIR OWN EMBLEM FOR CENTURIES. THE SWASTIKA IS REPRESENTATIVE OF THE SUN AND ITS RAYS.

Steeped in legend, the life of Zoroaster remains a tantalizing mystery. He was in his day as influential as Moses, as radical as Muhammad, and as dynamic as Jesus, yet few facts about his life can be established with any degree of certainty.

Some historians date his lifetime between 630 and 553 B.C., others place him firmly in the 10th century B.C., while yet another faction favors 1500 B.C. There are some who believe he did not ever live at all but was a composite character created entirely to expound the cause of a new-found religious movement.

ZOROASTER

THE PERSIAN PROPHET

It is thought he came from the eastern borders of present-day Iran, probably born to a priest and his wife. His family name was allegedly Spitama. Until Zoroaster —the Greek version of his Persian name, Zarathustra—was 30, he lived a predictable life. Then he began to seek enlightenment and had visions of God. It was through a vision that he learned of the existence of the Wise God whom he called Ahura Mazda, or Ohrmazd. Opposing Ahura Mazda was the Evil Spirit, Angra Mainyu, who vainly attempted to seduce Zoroaster. Zoroaster sought to live the "Good Life," as it became known, to win entry to heaven. He remained confident that good would always triumph over evil.

Delivering the good news about God cost Zoroaster his home and family. He was driven out of his community and wandered in the wilderness until he found his first convert, King Vishtaspa in eastern Persia. The protection of Vishtaspa enabled him to put his theology into practice with some degree of success.

However, the old rivalries were not ended. Zoroaster, it is said, was killed at the age of 77 by a sword-wielding priest from the old religion.

THUS SANG ZARATHUSTRA

Zoroaster's legacy was 17 songs, or *gathas*, contained in texts known as the *Yasna*. The contents of his writing reveal an evangelical zest for God and for life which remains an important part of Zoroastrianism today.

The hymns are the oldest part of the collected Zoroastrian scriptures called the *Avesta*, which include the *yasnas*, later hymns, or *yashts*, and a code of conduct, the *Vendidad*.

Zoroastrianism continued to develop even after Zoroaster's death. Wise men from Persia, some of whom featured in the Biblical tale of the birth of Jesus, became devotees and helped the cult survive. These Magi were star-gazers

wear masks so that their breath does not impinge on the sacred fires in Parsi temples. The devout pray five times daily.

The language for Parsi worship is ancient Persian. Temples are closed to non-believers. It is their belief that people should be content with the religion they were born into.

and observed magic rituals, too. Perhaps it was they who reintroduced significant ancient Persian gods to feature as lesser divinities.

The faith underwent mixed fortunes during the first centuries of the millennium, when its philosophies influenced the new religions of Islam and Christianity. It was all but squeezed out of Persia by Muslims in the 9th century.

Exiles left for India where the Hindus welcomed them. There they became known as Parsis, derived from the Indian word for Persian. Although a few Zoroastrians, known as Gabars, stayed in their homeland it was the Parsis who kept the word of Zoroaster alive.

ZOROASTRIAN TRADITIONS

Cleanliness is important to Parsis and they bathe before morning worship. A Parsi, like his high-caste Hindu counterpart, wears a sacred thread, or *kushti*, although his comprises 72 strands representing the chapters of the *Yasna*.

Worshippers wear a *sadre*, a shirt denoting their religion, while priests stand out because of their white robes and turbans. They also

One of the more remarkable departures from standard religious thought is the treatment of the dead. Rather than offend the elements with a corpse, Parsis put bodies in "Towers of Silence," or *dakhmas*, where they will be eaten by wild birds and animals. That is the purpose of the existence of the vulture, according to Parsi tradition.

Zoroastrians do not hold with eternal damnation. They believe souls will cross the narrow "Accountants' Bridge" on their way to heaven. If the good done in their life outweighs the evil, they will be escorted safely across by a beautiful woman. Should the opposite be true, an ugly hag greets them and they slip from the bridge into purgatory below where they will be purified in order to enter heaven at a later date.

"Piety is the best good. Happiness comes to him who shows the best piety." Parsi prayer.

CHAPTER SIX
BUDDHISM

The cold curves and blank-eyed stares of the Buddha statues which people the landscape of Southeast Asia, India, China, and beyond give away little about a religion which is many-layered and multi-faceted. To the uninitiated, the stone images of Buddha represent a mysterious god, awesome yet avuncular. However, Buddhism is a religion without a god, although its founder, the inspiration for the familiar statues, is venerated.

Buddhism is a religion of the interior. Meditation and contemplation are key for the Buddhist takes an inner journey not to God, but to bliss. It takes time and a not inconsiderable talent to achieve this. Observers define Buddhism as a philosophy and not a faith.

Ironically, Buddhism was all but extinguished in its homeland of India, but became established in its various forms in Nepal, Tibet, Vietnam, China, Korea, Japan, Sri Lanka, Burma, Thailand, Laos, and Kampuchea. It has attracted a following in the West, particularly among those who are disillusioned with the material world and seek an alternative. Some estimates put the number of Buddhists worldwide at 200 million. Others claim it is closer to one-third of the population of the globe.

"Once upon a time there was a beautiful queen called Maya who dreamt that she saw a white elephant with six tusks entering her side. Afterward she was overjoyed to find out that she was expecting a baby for she and the king had longed for a child. A strange voice then told how the son she would bear was to be a great world leader. Months later she gave birth painlessly in an idyllic park, clasping the branch of a tree, and the infant was caught in a golden net held by four gods. He was laid on a white lotus blossom. At once the baby rose up, took seven steps and announced, 'I am the chief in the world. This is my last birth. There is now no existence again.'"

THE STORY OF SIDDHARTHA

THE PHILOSOPHER PRINCE

You would be forgiven for thinking that the much-recounted story of how the Buddha was conceived and born was nothing more than a fairy tale. Nevertheless, that is how the Buddhist scriptures report the birth. Perhaps it was a fable concocted and embellished throughout the years to befit a man of the Buddha's standing. The tales handed down about the birth of important figures in religion seem prone to the most exotic exaggerations. However, the facts that we do know about his life, sketchy as they are, bear greater scrutiny.

The Buddha was born Siddhartha Gautama or Gotama in about 563 B.C. to royal and wealthy parents of the Sakya clan, a Hindu warrior caste. Siddhartha lived in splendor in the town of Kapilavastu in the foothills of the Himalayas and grew up to become an accomplished scholar and student of the martial arts. His mother, Maya, died a week after his birth and he was brought up by her sister, Maharprajapati, who later became queen by marrying Siddhartha's father, Suddhodana. Aged 16, Siddhartha married his cousin Yasodhara, a beautiful princess, who bore him a son, Rahula. Yet his life remained cloistered, for his father had been told by a seer that the boy would one day see four signs which would

radically change his life. Anxious that the royal line should continue, the king tried to keep his son from the forecast destiny.

Even within the confines of his palatial home Siddhartha became troubled by the human condition. When he was 29, he slipped away to sample life in the outside world. He encountered an old man, a sick man, a corpse being taken for cremation, and a shaven-headed holy man. The first three exhibited signs of suffering, while the fourth was marked by his inner peace and contentment. Siddhartha was deeply influenced by what he had seen and resolved to discover the cause and cure of such suffering. Under cover of darkness, he rode away from home on a horse, gave away his worldly belongings, shaved his head, and adopted the life of an ascetic.

"To the Buddha for refuge I go
To the Dhamma for refuge I go
To the Sangha for refuge I go"
Pilgrim chant.

SEXUAL EQUALITY

It was some 35 years before Siddhartha returned to be reconciled with his family. His affection for Maharprajapati, his aunt and stepmother, was still evident all those years later. He had decided on a men-only order for Buddhist monks, believing that a religion of men would last 1,000 years whereas one of mixed sexes would endure for only half that time. However, he changed his views and allowed the woman who had nurtured him to join a Buddhist community as a nun. Wisdom had prevailed as Buddhism, with its belief in equal opportunities, has now survived 2,500 years.

Far left: **The Buddha's footprints have become an enduring symbol of the faith. These decorated imprints are from the Damballa Caves, Sri Lanka.**

Left: **An 18th-century scroll from Nepal depicts the Buddha inaugurating the practice of receiving alms still exercised by monks today.**

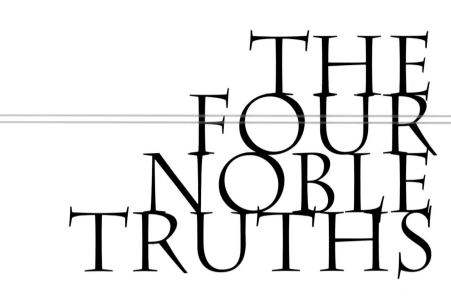

THE FOUR NOBLE TRUTHS

1. Human life is full of suffering, or *dukka*.

2. People themselves create this suffering by trying to cling on to worldly pleasures. The emergence of this craving is called *samodaya*.

3. If people set their feelings free and abandoned material hopes and dreams then suffering would end, a state of *nirodha*.

4. The Eightfold Path, or *magga*, is the route by which people can liberate themselves from suffering.

Siddhartha was absorbed by his quest for the truth behind the pitiful human condition. The burning questions of why people suffered and how that anguish could be alleviated were not easily answered.

Above: **The Sleeping Buddha in Sri Lanka. The Buddha sank into a deep trance before his death and the image of his last moments holds great significance for Buddhists.**

He visited Hindu teachers in pursuit of the necessary spiritual realization. Then he spoke to the yogis and hermits. However, no-one could offer a convincing theory. Following the example of five Brahmins he began to fast, becoming so thin that his ribs stuck out. After collapsing Siddhartha became convinced that such extremes of personal neglect were not the

way to achieve spiritual enlightenment. The Brahmins were so disappointed in his apparent display of human weakness that they abandoned him. For six years his painstaking search for enlightenment continued.

FROM TEMPTATION TO TRUTH

Sitting beneath a Bo tree (a pipal tree) on the banks of the River Gaya, Siddhartha meditated, determined to understand the truth. He was troubled by temptation offered by an evil spirit, Mara. When Siddhartha remained serene amidst an onslaught by an army of demons and the fury of inclement weather, Mara called up his three daughters, Lust, Restlessness, and Greed. All their efforts to distract the contemplation of the Buddha came to nothing.

After four weeks (some versions say seven) he was suffused by the great enlightenment. While his mind was suspended deep in meditation, the truth at last had crystallized for the Buddha. The soaring elation of discovering the truth was difficult to describe.

However, he realized that desire was the cause of much suffering and that self-denial could eliminate or tame it. Man could take the "Middle Way" between sensual indulgence and futile self-sacrifice. Before him Siddhartha saw the Four Noble Truths, the last being the Eightfold Path by which man could quell desire, and beyond that Nirvana, or spiritual peace. Thereafter he became the Gautama Buddha, the enlightened one. Once again that Mara appeared to him, imploring him to keep the Noble Truths secret. He refused.

Glowing with his new-found knowledge, the Buddha headed for Benares and on the way he encountered the Brahmins who had previously left him. Much against their judgment they listened to his words and were so stirred that they became his first converts.

WHEELS IN MOTION

His first sermon was delivered in a deer park near Benares. It has become known in Buddhist terms as *"The Discourse of the Setting in Motion of the Wheel of Dhamma"* or *Dhamma-cakkappa-vattana-sutta*, and its words have been preserved, although they were not put in writing until some years later.

The Buddha, otherwise known as "The Sage of the Sakyas," gathered converts as he traveled around the Ganges Valley. In the rainy season his followers, the Buddhists, lived in communities before once again taking advantage of sunny weather to spread their word of peace, piety, equality, and humility.

It was some 45 years later that the Buddha died, allegedly from poison. Some versions of his death have it that a poor blacksmith unknowingly fed him poisoned mushrooms while others claim he was deliberately killed by rotten meat. In any event he was 80 years old and content in the knowledge that the movement he had started was thriving and multiplying. Before his death he assumed the lotus position and voiced his final teachings to his most loyal disciples. Afterward, he lay on his right side and entered a deep meditation before passing away.

THE EIGHTFOLD PATH

To help his disciples win passage to Nirvana, the Buddha established an eight-point charter for living which would help his adherents put suffering behind them and achieve the necessary goodness and insight. The approach concentrated on morality, meditation, and wisdom.

1. Right views
2. Right thoughts
3. Right speech
4. Right action
5. Right occupation
6. Right effort
7. Right mindfulness
8. Right concentration

Above: **Compassion and generosity are the watchwords of the Buddhist faith. Accordingly, monks and nuns are able to live comfortably on the freely given charity of farmers and traders.**

THE RIGHT PATH TO NIRVANA

The Buddha urged his followers to have the "right views," that is to have a positive attitude about others as well as themselves. To achieve this entails a degree of faith in the words of the Buddha. With that comes the duty to consider the plight of others with sympathy and understanding and to back those "right thoughts" with "right speech," by never saying things that are hurtful or telling lies.

The "right action" is, of course, good conduct earned by not killing or maiming and not stealing the possessions of others. Good Buddhists will choose the "right occupation," a job that does not involve cheating on others or causing injury to anyone or anything. By following the Eightfold Path, Buddhists are making the "right effort" and living as the Buddha intended. "Right mindfulness" is awareness of the consequences of personal actions. Only by being aware can Buddhists halt a ripple effect, by which one action may affect other people. The "right concentration" is the tranquillity which they should find in pursuing the Eightfold Path.

A DISCIPLINED LIFESTYLE

In addition, the Buddha left a simple code which was named the Five Precepts. They reflect the nature of the Eightfold Path but are not its equivalent:

1. Be compassionate to all living things and do not harm or kill other people or animals.
2. Do not steal or take what has not been given. Always be generous to those in need.
3. Avoid alcohol and drugs because they cloud the mind.

"The doctrine and discipline which I have imparted to you will be your leader when I am gone. Try hard to reach the goal." The Buddha's last words.

4. Do not tell lies or say bad things about others.
5. Respect others and abstain from sexual immorality.

The first Precept explains why most Buddhists are vegetarian—to slaughter another animal for its meat is a contradiction of the teachings of the Buddha; the second Precept reveals why Buddhist monks and nuns are able to live without qualms upon community charity.

Only the most devout choose to follow the further three Precepts, those of refusing food after midday, abstaining from dancing and

Left: **Saffron robes distinguish the devoted followers of the Buddha, like this one studying the *Pali Canon* in Burma.**

Far left: **A 12th-century painting shows how Buddhist monks are willing to pass on the meager amounts of food they have to the poor.**

singing, and refusing to use garlands, jewelery, or make-up. Monks are subject to further codes which prevent them from taking gold and silver and using a bed.

A king once asked the Buddha what a monk needed to be happy. His reply was that he required food, freely given, a set of three robes, shelter for the night, and medicine for illness. The physical hardships of Buddhist monks may be immense but this is balanced by what they consider to be spiritual rewards.

CONCEPTS

To contemplate Buddhism is to delve deeply into philosophy and mysticism. However, to discuss Buddhist theory fully would require a book to itself, so a wander down the broad avenue of the Buddha's teachings rather than a tour of the side streets must suffice here. The Buddha himself was a great believer in the importance of experience over the word. He beckoned people with the phrase *"Ehi passiko!,"* or "come and see."

REBIRTH

One of his most challenging theories was that nothing remains the same. In death not only does the human body degenerate, but the soul also fragments, he declared. The elements of sensation, perception, volition, and consciousness starburst to mix and match with others and thus form new personalities. Hence the Buddhist phrase of *anatta*, meaning "no-self." The Buddha's aim was to explain why his disciples should obliterate their egos. He felt the only route to Nirvana was through abandoning the traditional views centered around the self in order to expand into a literally carefree existence. To explain: Nirvana is not a place like heaven, but its formless equivalent. It is an abstract realm of joy and eternal peace.

So reincarnation in Buddhist terms is not a return of the same soul in a different bodily guise, but a rebirth of a new combination representing the same life force. However, this rebirth is not a happy or desirable thing, associated as it is with bad *karma*—the negative thoughts, words, and actions delivered in the previous life. To transcend the wheel of rebirth one has to conquer desires, delusions, or hatred on earth and so attain Nirvana.

BODHISATTVAS

Not all Buddhists poised to reach Nirvana take the fateful step and leave the human world forever. Bodhisattvas are enlightened beings, ranking below Buddha status, but above ordinary mortals. Their compassion for the plight of others prevents them from entering Nirvana and instead they devote themselves to the redemption of others.

Bodhisattvas may be earthly Buddhists who have mastered the six perfections of charity, patience, vigor, meditation, wisdom, and morality. There are also those who are spiritual beings, similar to Christian saints, and they have in the past become the focus of cults.

Above: Commitment to a monastery need not be a lifelong pledge; it can be just for schooling.

Below left: Although Buddhism is a godless religion the faithful pay homage to Buddha at places like this shrine room in Sri Lanka.

"Whatever monks and divines in the future will enter upon and abide in a voidness that will be purified and unsurpassed by any other, they will all of them enter upon and abide in this voidness that is pure and unsurpassed by any other." From the *Culasunnata Sutra* of Theravadan Bhuddism, Thailand.

THE TWO VEHICLES OF BUDDHISM

Bodhisattvas are features of one of the two major branches of Buddhism. Mahãyãna Buddhism is the less severe interpretation of the Buddha's teachings, otherwise known as the "Great Vehicle," while Theravãda or the "Little Vehicle" is more rigid. In simple terms, the movement split soon after the death of the Buddha, with Theravãda doctrine insisting that only monks could achieve Nirvana. It remains the dominant form in Sri Lanka, Burma, Thailand, Laos, and Kampuchea. Mahãyãna Buddhism opens the door to all and has achieved the majority of followers.

While there has been sporadic rivalry between the two factions, for the most part communities live contentedly side by side. Tolerance is an important facet of Buddhism and has allowed the movement to spread among indigenous religions in Asia before finally incorporating them or some of their ideas.

The saffron-robed monks with their shaven heads are common to both strains of Buddhism, as are the nuns or devout women. Unlike Christian monks and nuns, they are not bound to the order, or *sangha*, for life. Some might enter for a limited time, say a year, for their spiritual merit. It is usual for boys to spend at least a week in a monastery as part of their religious education.

Gautama believed himself to be the seventh Buddha and that others would follow.

Although the Buddhas are not gods, they are the subject of devotion by monks, nuns, and pilgrims. When the Buddha died, his ashes were divided between eight groups who kept them in cairns, or *stupas*. Eventually the *stupas* evolved into *pagodas*, the familiar shrines of Southeast Asia today. Perhaps the most famous is the Golden Pagoda in Rangoon, more than 300 feet high and covered entirely with gold leaf. Its Buddha images are hewn from a further 25 tons of gold and it is topped by an umbrella decorated with more than 4,000 diamonds. Inside are said to be the hairs of Siddhartha, as well as the sandals and robes of former Buddhas. Relics and other reminders of the Buddha, for example the Bo tree, are used in worship. They are seen as being inspirational rather than as idols.

As in other religions, Buddhism spread by word of mouth and the teachings of the Buddha were handed down from generation to generation. Only after several centuries was the *Dhamma* recorded in the North Indian language of Pali. Consequently the holy book of Buddhism became known as the *Pali Canon*.

Ashoka fostered many religions, but was particularly supportive of Buddhism. Consequently the tradition of missionary work to the far corners of his extensive domain began, continuing beyond the borders after his death. Different schools of Buddhism developed, but all came under the same religious umbrella.

It took less than three centuries for Buddhism to filter into China. However, it was not until the 6th century, with the arrival of an Indian Buddhist monk called Bodhidharma, that the religion began to get a foothold. There is much speculation about his position in the spiritual hierarchy, with some believing he was already an Enlightened One. Legend has it that he meditated for nine years facing a wall, rendering his withered legs useless.

THE BIRTH OF ZEN

Then came Hui-neng (A.D. 637–713), the man widely credited with the founding of Zen Buddhism, the most popular sect in China and Japan and latterly the West.

Hui-neng coined the phrase which so aptly sums up Zen Buddhism, "seeing into one's own nature." He taught that everyone was born

ZEN BUDDHISM AND THE DALAI LAMAS

For the spread of the Buddha's word from its Indian home to surrounding countries history has one man to thank—Emperor Ashoka (273–232 B.C.) turned to Buddhism after conducting a particularly violent campaign of acquisition. So appalled was he at the bloodletting, that he decreed that the drums of war would henceforth be replaced by the chants of the *Dhamma* in his kingdom.

pure and had therefore achieved enlightenment. It was merely a case of recognizing that fact. Students have been quick to point out the influence of Chinese religions on Buddhism as it traveled east and resulted in the hybrid of Zen.

In Japanese history, key Zen Buddhists are the monk Ei-sai (A.D. 1141–1215) founder of the Rinzai sect in 1191, and Dogen (A.D. 1200–1253), creator of the Soto sect. Dogen remains a prominent figure to Zen Buddhists, although his favored mode of silent meditation differed from the Rinzai preference for *koan*, paradoxes which are repeated until enlightenment prevails. There are around 1,700 *koan* and they present imponderables such as: "What was your true face before your mother and father were born?"

Its very title, Zen, can be roughly translated to mean meditation. Zen is the Japanese version of a Chinese word, *Ch'an*, which in itself was a translation of the Sanskrit word *dhyana*. Its spread in Japan was fortuitous as the faith was able to prosper even after the anti-religious Mongols invaded China in the 12th century.

ACHIEVING SATORI

The ambition of practitioners is to achieve enlightenment, or *satori*, through meditation. Usually the lotus position is adopted—crossed

Left: To Buddhists life is seen as a wheel, this one being turned by Yama, the Lord of Death. The aim is to leave the wheel entirely.

legs with feet resting on opposite thighs or stomach. The eyes are open and looking downward, while the hands join to form an oval resting against the abdomen. In Zen it is known as *Zazen*.

Some students find consultation with a teacher, or *roshi*, is helpful in the pursuit of enlightenment. The *roshi* is unlikely to eulogize over the wonders of enlightenment. The emphasis is on doing it rather than talking about it. *Satori* is ultimately honed until a state of "no-mind" or "no-thought" occurs, bringing the clarity of vision of enlightenment.

THE YELLOW HATS

In Tibet there is another face of Buddhism reflecting how, once exported, it absorbed the indigenous religion already in existence.

Tsong-Kapa, a teacher, (A.D. 1357–1417) initiated a sect known as the Gelug-pa, the Yellow Hats. They were highly disciplined and morally sound and they very quickly predominated over the existing Red Hats who were somewhat lax. A much-admired abbot who died in 1475 was believed to have been reincarnated in the form of a young monk. The cycle

Left: **Richard Gere, star of "An Officer and a Gentieman" and confirmed Buddhist, meets the Dalai Lama.**

was repeated and Tibetans believed that the chosen monks, or Dalai Lamas, were actually the living embodiment of the spiritual Bodhisattva, Avalokitesvara.

By 1642 the Yellow Hats ruled Tibet, with the Dalai Lama at their head. For centuries the Dalai Lama remained the head of state, but in 1959 an uprising against the ruling Chinese was crushed, and he and his followers fled. Since then he has been a leader-in-exile. The Panchen Lama, or chief abbot of Tashilhunpo monastery at Zhikatse, who ranks second to the Dalai Lama, remained. He is said to be a reincarnation of Amitabha, the Buddha of Infinite Light. Tibetan Buddhism is also known as Lamaism.

CHR

CHAPTER SEVEN
CHRISTIANITY

Christianity has grown from the extraordinary talents of one man, Jesus, who lived 2,000 years ago, into the largest religion in the world today with some 1,700 million followers. If the story of his life is compelling, it is the manner of his death and the events after it that laid the foundations of the faith.

It is Jesus's death and his consequent resurrection, symbolizing the triumph of good over evil, upon which Christianity is based. The central element of the Christian faith, unlike any other, is the suffering endured by its Messiah, intertwined with mystic symbolism.

THE STORY OF JESUS

Every Christmas, the story of Mary and Joseph traveling to Bethlehem for a census and bedding down for the night in a stable when there was no room at the inn brings a cosy glow to listeners. There are shepherds, lambs, wise men, and angels to embellish the tale.

THE COMING OF THE KING

Few question the facts—there was no census taken at the time or, indeed, until Jesus was about nine years old; nor do the Gospels mention a stable in their accounts of Christ's birth—a cave is more likely. Nevertheless, the story is passed from generation to generation.

This is just a glimpse of the difficulties facing scholars who seek to define Jesus the man from Jesus the myth. While the Gospels must be the key source, they were written some years after his death. At best they were second-hand or anecdotal accounts, and were all written by Christians who believed in Jesus and wanted to glorify him. Jesus did not bequeath his teachings in written form, at least, none that are known.

Perhaps the arguments over dates overshadow what really matters about the life of Jesus—that his teachings are the basis of modern Western society and that his life emphasized the need for less of the piety and asceticism which obsess other cults, and more charity, love, and social justice.

To study the impact that Jesus made, we must first look at the place and time in which he lived. Jesus grew up in Galilee, where his father Joseph was a carpenter. Galilee is green and pleasant. Despite plentiful winter rainfall, the soil is stony rather than richly fertile. It is a land of vines, olives, almonds, palms, and pomegranates. The River Jordan snakes its way from the Sea of Galilee, a long-time focus for the fishing industry, down to the barren and salty Dead Sea in the south.

Jesus was born into a Jewish family, he attended the synagogue, and picked his disciples from the Jewish community. Given the Roman occupation of the region, and what was perceived to be a laxity in religious observance, the Jewish religion was subject to divisions and factions. There were the Pharisees, strict and severe in their interpretation of Jewish law; the equally ardent Hasidim, or "pious ones;" the Sadducees and the Essenes, both Old Testament purists; and the Zealots, militants opposed to the Romans. The Scribes were the lawyers and teachers or rabbis.

Although many miles from his home at Nazareth, Jesus went to the capital city, Jerusalem, for major religious festivals. He spoke Aramaic, a language now found only in a small Christian corner of Syria, but was probably acquainted with Greek, the official tongue of the Roman Empire. Indeed, the very word Christ, "the anointed one," has its roots in the Greek language.

Some believe Jesus was an illegitimate child, born from Mary's liaison with a Roman soldier, that he was born in a cave as Joseph was too humiliated to present the pregnant Mary as his fiancée, that he used his divine/supernatural powers to both entertain and torture playmates, that he was insolent to his teachers, that he traveled to England aboard a ship as a wheelwright. For the most part, these are taken from apocryphal Gospels and their authenticity is doubtful.

Above: **The idyllic scene of Christ's birth has long been an inspiration to artists.**

Left: **Jerusalem was already a holy city for Jews at the time of Jesus. It was to become so for Christians and Muslims, too.**

REBEL WITH A CAUSE

Jesus was something of a rebel in an era when rebellion was remorselessly crushed. His concerns were not with the laws of the appointed church elders, but with those of God. Hypocrisy was clearly annoying and Jesus famously entered the temple to overturn the tables of the moneylenders, so alien was their activity to the original purpose of the place of worship.

There are celebrated incidents in the Gospels:

—Aged 12, Jesus slipped away from Joseph and Mary during a visit to Jerusalem for Passover and was found days later discussing religion with temple elders.

—When Jesus was baptized in the Jordan by John the Baptist, a heavenly voice declared, "Thou art my beloved son. In thee I am well pleased."

—Afterward, Jesus went into the desert to fast for 40 days and nights, resisting temptation by the devil, before returning to start his ministry which lasted less than four years.

—Jesus taught that the way to salvation was through love of God and man. He emphasized the value of charity, humility, repentance, and forgiveness and kept the company of society's outcasts to prove his point.

—His miracles included restoring sight to the blind, speech to the dumb, hearing to the deaf. He cured those suffering from leprosy, epilepsy, demonic possession, and paralysis, and, on three occasions, he raised the dead.

The persuasive words of Jesus's preaching and the miracles he performed galvanized the local population. He called into question the wisdom and merit of the existing religious hierarchy and soon the religious leaders collaborated in order to rid themselves of this irritant.

Jesus realized what fate held in store. After all, John the Baptist had already been arrested and executed.

While the words of Jesus were compelling, it was the miracles he performed that were the crowd-pleasers. These included restoring sight to the blind, speech to the dumb, and hearing to the deaf. He cured those suffering from leprosy, epilepsy, demonic possession, and paralysis and, on three occasions, he raised the dead. The miracles were seen as God's work on earth carried out through Jesus.

THE MIRACLES

The first of the miracles, according to the Gospel of John, occurred at Cana during a wedding at which Jesus was a guest. His mother Mary noticed the wine was running low. Jesus ordered the servants to replenish the jugs with water. But when they were poured out it was the best wine that flowed. Jesus was reluctant to intervene, telling his mother "mine hour is not yet come." However, for the disciples who accompanied him to the feast it was just an inkling of his extreme greatness.

Three miracles took place on or by the Sea of Galilee. According to Matthew, a tempest overtook the ship on which Jesus and his disciples were traveling. Terrified for their lives, the men woke Jesus who had been sleeping. "'Why are ye fearful, O ye of little faith?' Then he arose, and rebuked the winds and the sea; and there was a great calm."

Jesus once again revealed a mastery over the forces of nature to soothe the anxieties of his disciples during stormy weather by walking

"At sunset all those who had friends suffering from diseases of one kind or another brought them to him, and laying hands on each he cured them." *Luke 4:40*

Above: Artist Juan de Flanders (1496–c.1519) was moved by the story of the resurrection of Lazarus to paint this masterpiece.

Right: After intervention by Jesus, fishermen on the Sea of Galilee landed an enormous catch when before their nets were empty. By Konrad Witz (1400–1445).

upon the water. This occurred after he had fed, with just five loaves and two fishes, the 5,000 people who came to listen to him preach in a desert. The remainders of the divine feast filled a dozen baskets.

One of those raised from the dead was the son of a widow at Nain. So moved was Jesus by the weeping of his mother that he touched the funeral bier and said, "Young man, I say unto thee, Arise." The 12-year-old daughter of the synagogue elder Jairus was likewise restored to life (both incidents are related in Luke's Gospel), while Jesus raised his friend Lazarus after the latter had been dead for four days. Crowds had gathered to comfort Mary and Martha, the sisters of Lazarus. According to John's Gospel, "Then many of the Jews which came to Mary and had seen the things which Jesus did, believed in him."

News was always spread by word of mouth, there being no newspapers, mail, or telephones, so the happenings were reported across the region by witnesses to their family and friends. The more who saw the miracles—and frequently there were many in the vicinity when they occurred—the greater Jesus's reputation became. Consequently, he was often pursued by mighty crowds and many in the throng were ill. On one occasion a sick man was lowered through the roof of a house in order to reach Jesus. Despite the pressures that his popularity entailed, Jesus was almost always sympathetic with their plight.

> "And Jesus went forth and saw a great multitude, and was moved with compassion toward them, and he healed their sick." *Matthew 14:14*

Just to touch the hem of his garment was proven to be enough to heal the faithful. In the 2,000 years since these miracles occurred, there has been no explanation as to how they were carried out, save that proffered by Jesus himself, that he was working as the implement of God. So many miraculous stories are related in the Gospels that to have imagined it could only be a case of mass hallucination or a kind of collective hysteria.

Above: Jesus would not let a faithful crowd starve. Accordingly, he fed the 5,000 who flocked to see him with just five loaves of bread and two fishes. By Hendrick de Clerck (1570–1629).

Healers have come and gone since Jesus's time, leaving behind some converts and believers, as well as a number of sceptics. In the past century, the number of self-acclaimed healers has risen dramatically. Some remarkable results have been documented, but there has been no scientific study to determine whether or not the "cures" are long-lasting. Many healers, such as Edgar Cayce (1877–1945), are confirmed Christians. And, like Jesus, Cayce declined any money for his services, until, that is, he gave up his photographer's job because the weight of work as a psychic healer became too great.

He demanded faith in God from his patients, much the same as Jesus before him. It leads the impartial observer to conclude that some unknown mental forces must be at work and mind over matter is playing its part. To reinforce this message Cayce's favorite phrase was, "Mind is the builder."

CHRIST AS A SYMBOL OF FAITH

At the Passover feast of A.D. 29 or 30, Jesus and his 12 disciples gathered somberly while the rest of the city commemorated the Exodus of the Jews from Egypt. Jesus predicted that one of the 12 would betray him and that Peter would deny him three times before the cock crowed the next morning.

What happened next is one of the most significant events in Jesus's life, pivotal in the ensuing success of Christianity. Jesus blessed and broke the bread and gave it to his disciples, saying, "Take, eat, this is my body."

Then he passed around the red wine, declaring, "This is my blood . . . shed for many for the remission of sins."

It is this act that became the foundation of the Eucharist, or Holy Communion.

Jesus was arrested following his betrayal by Judas. Sensing danger, his disciples ran off and Peter duly denied three times before dawn that he was an associate of the arrested man.

THE CRUCIFIXION

Jesus was accused of blasphemy by the high priests, convicted and taken in chains to Pontius Pilate, the Roman governor. He hoped he would be released as part of the Passover celebrations, but the mob chose another condemned man, Barabbas, for the reprieve and Jesus was crucified.

Crucifixion was agonizing and reserved for the lowliest criminals as a particularly demeaning way to die. Victims were flogged and then forced to walk to the scene of their impending death dragging the beam of the cross on which they would die. (The full weight of the cross would have been too much to bear.) So shame-

Left: **Jesus had valued women companions— unusual for the era. One, Mary Magdalene, is depicted here by Luca Signorelli (1441–1523) grieving at his crucifixion.**

> "Go forth therefore and make all nations my disciples; baptize men everywhere in the name of the Father and the Son and the Holy Spirit, and teach them to observe all that I have commanded you. And be assured, I am with you always, to the end of time." Jesus speaks to his disciples after his resurrection. *Matthew 28:19–20*

ful was his death that it took Jesus's followers years to accept the symbol of him on the cross as a sign of their faith. A notice detailing the felon's name and crime was pinned to the top. In Jesus's case it apparently read INRI, *Iesus Nazarenus Rex Iudaeorum*, Jesus of Nazareth, King of the Jews. Death was mercilessly slow.

With a crown of thorns on his head and a baying crowd beneath, the humiliation of Jesus was complete. At noon that Friday, darkness cloaked the land for three hours. Famously, Jesus cried out before his death, "My God, my God, why hast thou forsaken me?" At his last breath, the curtain in the temple was torn in two and the area struck by an earthquake.

To his followers, it seemed that Jesus's life and works had miserably failed. The taunt that he had saved others but could not save himself, rang true. However, the death of Jesus, brutal though it appeared, represented a reconciliation between man and God, known as atonement, or "at-one-ment." Man was therefore redeemed, despite his history of sin.

THE RESURRECTION

That evening, the wealthy Joseph of Arimathea won permission to claim Jesus's body. He wrapped it in a shroud and put it in a tomb, which was covered by a large boulder. Soldiers guarded the entrance, fearing the body would be snatched by extremist followers.

On Sunday Mary Magdalene and other women disciples found the tomb empty and were told by an angel that Jesus had been raised. Until they saw him with their own eyes, the disciples were sceptical. The sight of him reinforced their beliefs. For 40 days Jesus appeared to his faithful followers, numbering as many as 500, before he ascended to God, the mortal man having become immortal.

Claims abound that Jesus's body remained on earth. In 1996, two British men, Paul Schellenberger and Richard Andrews, reported that the remains of the Messiah could be found on the side of a French mountain. They came to their conclusions after studying geometric patterns on ancient manuscripts and paintings and linking them to the Knights Templar, mysterious Christian soldiers who fought in the Middle East, but also had a base nearby.

The same year found a TV crew in Jerusalem pondering over the significance of a group of caskets kept in a warehouse dating back to the 1st century A.D., which bore, among others, the names of Joseph, Mary, and Jesus. Despite the fact that they were common names, it was a perplexing issue.

Left: **Christ is often seen in terms of the Lamb of God. Here the lamb bears the banner of the crucifixion, now the common symbol of the resurrection.**

Today medical science is certain when death occurs, but it was not so then. Families of convicted felons often stood by in the hope of reviving their loved ones after execution. The rational mind cannot help but wonder if Jesus died at all and whether he was merely unconscious and later recovered. There's even one school of thought that says the crucifixion was an elaborate hoax.

However, challengers of the resurrection story have failed to yield any conclusive evidence. At a time when archeology confirms many of the Bible stories, it will take more than a fleeting theory to shake 2,000 years of faith.

These were not the bravest, strongest, cleverest, or most wealthy of men. They were picked for their faith, which wavered at times during the life of Jesus, but, most importantly, never faltered after his death.

THE DISCIPLES

When Jesus began his ministry time was short and the task of spreading the Word of God was immense, so he recruited 12 disciples to assist. Significantly, the number of disciples mirrored the number of Jewish tribes that entered Israel. The dozen, together with Matthias (who replaced Judas Escariot) and St. Paul, were later known, along with other Christian missionaries, as Apostles.

Above: **A 12th-century painting of the Apostles Peter and Andrew at work as fishermen, pictured on the ceiling of St. Martin's Church at Zillis, Switzerland.**

What most convinced them about Jesus was his ability to perform miracles. From Luke's Gospel we hear how the fisherman Peter was recruited. He had landed nothing, but on Jesus's instructions cast his net once more, and the catch was so mighty that it almost sank the boat. "When Peter saw it he fell down at Jesus's knee, saying, 'Depart from me, for I am a sinful man, O Lord.' And Jesus said: 'Fear not; from henceforth thou shalt catch men.'"

Until he became a follower of Jesus, Matthew was a *telones*, or high-ranking tax collector, a profession despised by the Jews, who saw such officials as collaborators with the Roman occupation forces. Before his martyrdom he preached in Judea and then overseas in Ethiopia and Persia.

Following the death of Jesus, his disciples were filled with the Holy Spirit, a divine fervor. Accompanying it came the gift of speaking in different tongues (languages) which endorsed their loyalty and commitment to Christ and enabled them to communicate with the many races of the region.

ST. PAUL

It was Saul, later St. Paul, who was the key to the spread of Christianity from the region of Israel to the rest of civilization. Paul was a Roman citizen of Jewish faith from the city of Tarsus in Turkey. He was a Pharisee—and therefore not well disposed toward the burgeoning Christian movement—until his famous conversion to Christianity on the road to Damascus. His success then came by preaching about a living Christ, rather than one who had died on a cross. Thus he won over many Jews who would otherwise have been less than happy to know that their rabbis had

called for the obliteration of God's own son. He felt it was his duty to carry the word of the Jewish Jesus to fellow Jews. When he encountered continuing hostility from the synagogues, he decided to speak to the Gentiles, or non-Jews, instead.

Like John the Baptist and Jesus before him, St. Paul rankled the Jewish authorities enough to be arrested. As a Roman citizen he elected for trial in Rome and it was there he died in about A.D. 63, probably at the hands of Nero. Peter was also martyred there and the two became widely regarded as the founders of the Roman Catholic church.

As the word of Christ was channeled through Jewish synagogues, and they were already in existence in prominent centers such as Alexandria, Rome, and Carthage, Christianity spread at speed.

The Apostles were ably assisted by traders who transported ideas, along with their silks and fancy goods, from place to place. Slaves, too, adopted the beliefs of Christianity, traveling between Christian colonies which sprang up all over the Roman empire.

The 12 Apostles were: Andrew, Bartholomew (or Nathaniel), James,son of Alphaeus, James, son of Zebedee, John, Jude (or Thaddeus), Judas Escariot, Matthew (or Levi), Philip, Peter, Simon the Zealot, and Thomas. After Judas Escariot killed himself, he was replaced by Matthias. St. Paul is included because he claimed to have seen Jesus after the resurrection.

"Ye men of Galilee, why stand ye gazing up into heaven?" *Acts of the Apostles 11*

The Bible is more than just a book, it is the equivalent of a whole shelf of books. There are 66 separate books, varying in age and length. The first 39 are collectively known as the Old Testament, while the rest belong to the New Testament.

THE BIBLE

THE OLD TESTAMENT

It is important to Jews and Christians alike. Both had to be content with a 9th century A.D. version. But in 1947 a Bedouin Arab boy hurled a stone into a cave and heard something shatter. On investigation he found a collection of clay jars, each of which held manuscript scrolls beautifully preserved in linen covers. It was later discovered that they had once belonged to the Essenes monks, but were probably secreted away during a Roman purge. The date of these manuscripts was estimated at A.D. 70.

In fact, the wording of the Dead Sea Scrolls and their 9th-century descendants had changed little. The name of God, which was considered too holy to be written, was symbolized by four dots. The discovery revealed that Jesus would have been well versed in the same Old Testament that we know today.

THE FOUR GOSPELS

The New Testament is the story of Jesus's life and works. Matthew, Mark, Luke, and John are credited for the four Gospels, although historians have cast doubt upon the authorship.

First to be written was "Mark's Gospel," which is dated at around A.D. 65–70. Mark accompanied Paul to Rome and acted as an interpreter there for Peter.

Chronologically, Matthew is next, written using "Mark's Gospel" as a source. It gives a Jewish perspective, showing Jesus as the Old Testament's promised Messiah.

Little is known about Luke. A Gentile doctor who worked with St. Paul on missions to Greece, Macedonia, and Jerusalem, he was led by both Mark and Matthew. His is the fullest account of Jesus's birth. Material not found in Mark but evident in both Matthew and Luke is believed to have come from a lost source, known as Q.

The fourth Gospel was for centuries believed to have been written by John but is now thought to be the work of another. Its content differs from the other three in that it is less a description of Jesus's life and more an interpretation of his work.

There are further books in the New Testament including the "Acts of the Apostles" and 21 epistles or letters sent by St. Paul and others to churches and friends. It concludes with the book of "Revelation" or "Apocalypse" featuring strange, nightmarish visions.

THE BIBLE THROUGH THE AGES

Today's New Testament is based on parchment copies made of the originals in the 4th century. One such copy is called the *Vaticanus* and resides in the Vatican library in Rome, while another, the *Sinaiticus*, discovered in the 19th century at St. Catherine's monastery on Mount Sinai, is in the British Museum.

Fragments of papyrus bought by an obscure clergyman in Egypt at the beginning of the 20th century have been dated as being from A.D. 65 or before and appear to contain the Gospel according to Matthew. They may be all we have left of an original Gospel. If this is true, it could be that Matthew's account is within 30 years of Jesus's death and based on eyewitness accounts.

How the writings were drawn together is not entirely clear. However, it is known that by A.D. 200 the four Gospels of Matthew, Mark, Luke, and John had been accepted, while others were rejected. "Revelation" was one of the last books to join the fold.

"No man, who knows nothing else, knows even his Bible." Matthew Arnold, *Culture and Anarchy (1869)*

TRANSLATIONS AND REVISIONS

The New Testament was standardized by Jerome on Pope Damasus's orders in A.D. 384 and his version, the *Vulgate*, or Common Version, remains the accepted authority by the Roman Catholic church. Scholars have since pored over available manuscripts to evolve the most accurate version of the New Testament.

John Wyclif translated the New Testament into English in 1384 and Martin Luther completed his German version by 1532. William Tyndale and Myles Coverdale earned themselves notoriety with their English translations, but were vindicated when much of their work appeared in the influential King James (Authorized) Version, which appeared in 1611 after being selected by a team of scholars.

Numerous revisions and translations have taken place to make the Bible accessible to all. *The Good News Bible*, a product of the American Bible Society in 1966, uses modern phraseology without losing the essential message. By 1984 the Bible had been translated into 586 languages and Bible Societies continue the work of translation.

Left: The Dead Sea scrolls were discovered here at Qumran, northwest of the Dead Sea, by chance. In total 500 different documents were recovered from 11 caves dating from 250 B.C. to A.D. 70, probably the library of the Essenes community.

THE EARLY YEARS

Judaism had won for itself the tolerance of the Roman authorities and Jews were able to observe the Sabbath and maintain the temple without fear of persecution. At first, Christians were regarded as a Jewish sect and as such were left in peace.

However, increasing numbers of Gentiles boosted the body of Christians to alarming proportions. Even the lofty Roman rulers could not fail to notice the hostility with which the Jews greeted the Christians. Clearly, Christians were a breed apart.

When Christians in Rome refused to worship the Roman gods they earned the enmity of the locals. Consequently, the followers of this new faith would meet in secret and at night. Wild rumors circulated about their behavior, said to include orgies, incest, and cannibalism. The latter accusation almost certainly grew out of the Eucharist in which the body of Christ in the form of bread or a wafer is consumed—a difficult practice to adequately explain then, it remains so today.

PERSECUTION

In the year A.D. 64, Rome burned and some believed that Nero, the mad emperor, had sparked the devastating blaze. His scapegoats were to be the Christians, as the historian Tacitus explained:

"Mockery of every sort was added to their deaths. Covered with the skins of beasts they were torn by dogs and perished; or were nailed to crosses; or were doomed to the flames."

It was this wave of anti-Christian feeling that probably claimed the lives of both St. Peter and St. Paul. The growing number of Christians, drawn generally from the lower echelons of society, periodically suffered under subsequent emperors. The Emperor Gaius Decius (201–51 A.D.) brought with him a dangerous age. He came to power in A.D. 249 and was fired by the celebrations of one thousand years of the Roman empire. His aim was to see Roman gods reinstated as vital symbols of a venerated culture and rival deities were to be expunged. Bishop Fabian of Rome was executed while other prominent Christians preferred exile.

Far left: Constantinople, which straddles the Bosphorus, became one of the key centers of Christianity. Before A.D. 330, it was known as Byzantium. Since 1926 its official name has been the Muslim one of Istanbul.

Left: Constantine the Great was a convert from Mithraism and became the first Christian Roman Emperor. To the discomfort of pious clerics, he began a trend which had Roman rulers depicted at God's right hand with the attributes of saints.

The Christians who remained to stand by their faith were thereafter known as the confessors, while those who switched to Roman ways for the duration of Decius's reign were known as "the lapsed." Decius was killed by the Goths, but like-minded emperors stepped into his shoes.

Peace came in 312 following the defeat by Constantine the Great (c.280–337) of Maxentius, the Roman challenger for the emperor's seat, at the Battle of Milvan Bridge. Twelve years later he vanquished the Eastern emperor Lincinius, becoming master of a mighty empire straddling the Mediterranean and reaching far beyond it.

THE CHRISTIAN EMPIRE

More crucially for the infant Christian religion, he was a convert. Constantine had worshipped the sun god. Before his military victories, he saw a vision in the sun featuring the letters CH and R and the words "*In boc signo vinces,*" or "In this sign shalt thou conquer." Constantine believed the message came from the Christian God and, with successes stacking up, he became the first Christian emperor. He turned the town of Byzantium into the great city of Constantinople and thus Christianity held an important stake in eastern Europe and Asia. After Jerusalem and Rome, Constantinople became the third most important city in Christendom.

The religion became identified as much with the ruler of the Christian empire as with Jesus himself. Christian art had the emperor depicted at Christ's right hand, complete with halo, with bishops clearly subordinate. Constantine, who was baptized on his deathbed, propelled the religion away from its humble roots to the very top of the social hierarchy and spanning all things in between.

He began a tradition of building ornate houses of worship, borrowing the idea from Persia where domes were grand and bejeweled.

Tolerance of Christians soon turned into active encouragement, which included tax concessions, followed by penalties for non-believers. In 380 the Emperor Theodosius decreed that Christianity was to be the religion of the empire.

He commanded, "It is our will that all the peoples we rule shall practice that religion which the divine Peter the Apostle transmitted to the Romans. We shall believe in the single deity of the Father, the Son, and the Holy Spirit, under the concept of equal majesty and of the Holy Trinity . . ."

So taken with the faith was Theodosius that he gave himself a new title of the "the visible God." To the discomfort of the learned and pious clerics, the Church and the state became one.

"The Christians are a class of men given to a new and wicked superstition." Suetonius (Roman historian, c.70–c.140).

"There is no such thing as Jew and Greek, slave and freeman, male and female; for you are all one in Christ Jesus." St. Paul.

EAST-WEST SCHISM

The Church struggled to consolidate its powers. But before the religion—which now encompassed many races, nations, and creeds—could unify, it was split apart by bitter disputes.

The topic that would rent the Church in two was the confusing philosophical point about the relationship of Jesus to God. Was he divine or semi-divine? Had he always existed or was he created? If there was only one God, what was the exact position of Jesus and the Holy Spirit in the celestial hierarchy?

The first General Council of the Church, which met at Nicea in A.D. 325 at the command of Constantine, attempted to resolve the row. The Nicene Creed sought to explain the role of Jesus the Son and was adopted as part of the Eucharist. An article known as the Filioque was added much later and rejected by the Patriarch of Constantinople. The Filioque dealt with the problem of the Holy Spirit by describing it as coming from "the Father and the Son" rather than from the Father alone. Although the article was adopted in Rome, Constantinople was offended at the challenge to God's sole authority. Church councils were the accepted way of resolving differences, although often unsuccessfully.

In 451, at the Council of Chalcedon, the balance of power in the Christian Church was addressed. Five seats of authority were declared at Constantinople, Rome, Jerusalem, Alexandria, and Antioch. The Roman bishops saw themselves as descendants of St. Peter and thus claimed the moral high ground. Even so, the Bishop of Constantinople appointed for himself the title of Ecumenical Patriarch. The mutual distrust between the two centers continued to deepen.

In the 6th century the Monophysites found themselves isolated by their creed, that there was "one nature" alone in Christ. They split to form the Syrian, Armenian, and Coptic (Egyptian) Churches. This led to further divisions within the Christian Church.

ORTHODOX CHURCHES

When the Frankish king Charlemagne was crowned by Pope Leo III in Rome and the influence of the Holy Roman Empire began to rise, Constantinople was outraged. The dispute between the city, now suffering declining fortunes, and its Italian rival finally boiled over in 1054 when the Patriarch of Constantinople was excommunicated, permanently dividing the Catholic Church and Orthodox Church.

Constantinople was eventually invaded by Muslims and Christianity became a minority religion. Yet the Greek Orthodox religion,

although beaten back to its country's borders, flourished and was exported with its emigrants. The Eastern Orthodox Churches remained a federation, with individual Patriarchs referring back to the Ecumenical Patriarch.

More crucially, the Russian people took Orthodoxy to their hearts—King Boris of Bulgaria converted in the 9th century and Russian ruler Vladimir was baptized in 988. It was apparently the splendor of Orthodox churches that converted Vladimir. Russian Orthodox churches, soon in the majority, split from the Greeks in the 15th century. The gold domes of Moscow and other Russian cities were the centuries-long mark of a religion inextricably linked to the state and its rulers. The Communists who seized power in Russia were understandably at odds with a religion with such a lavish image. Despite their efforts, Russian Orthodoxy could not be silenced and, like its Greek cousin, it went overseas and flourished, claiming to be the One True Church.

In addition to the ancient Patriarchs, there are ruling bishops in Moscow, Georgia, Serbia, Bulgaria, and Romania, as well as Cyprus, Albania, the Czech Republic, and Poland. Orthodoxy does not demand celibacy from its clergy and, while three-dimensional images are banned, the worship of icons is an important facet. Its liturgies are the work of St. John Chrysostom and St. Basil, and are sung without accompaniment.

The fortunes of Rome ebbed and flowed in the first thousand years of Christendom. After the glories of the Roman Empire, which began

CATHOLICISM

long before the time of Jesus, invaders came who sacked the capital and seized its riches. Some, like the Visigoths who struck in 410, were Christian by inclination, but most who breached the borders of the empire were not.

Yet Christianity remained secure and predominant thanks to the efforts of men like St. Leo the Great. As spiritual leader of the Western end of the Christian empire between 440 and 461, he made treaties with invading Huns and Vandals which protected Rome from their onslaught. Rome's bishops claimed to be the successors of the Apostle Peter, Christ's deputy, and accordingly commanded utmost respect. One was elected as a Patriarch. The term Pope was not formally used until 1073.

The strength of the faith was spiritual, as no Christian could quarrel with God's authority. On earth, however, the behavior of God's representatives was often distinctly unchristian and, even after the East-West schism, the Catholic Church was still bubbling with divisions.

CHARLEMAGNE

St. Leo III was physically attacked by fellow churchmen following his election as Patriarch in 795. Ejected from Rome in 799, he sought the assistance of Charlemagne, the Christian King of the Franks, who had done much to spread the word of Christianity. He offered the nationals of the countries he had invaded the opportunity to convert—or die. Leo was duly returned in glory to Rome and Charlemagne

Above: **Originally a Jewish practice, confession was adopted by Christianity and became obligatory from 1215. "The Confession" by Pietro Longhi (1702–1785).**

was crowned king of the Holy Roman Empire in A.D. 800.

The Holy Roman Empire was the natural successor to the old Roman Empire and, when Charlemagne's line failed, authority went to the German kings. However, they did not achieve the dominance over the papacy that their predecessors had enjoyed.

Any threats of earthly might that could be wielded against papal power were swiftly counteracted by the weapon of excommunication. When King John of England clashed with Pope Innocent III in 1205 over the pivotal

Above: "The Communion" by Francis Wheatley (1747–1801).

Left: The Avignon papacy is often referred to as the Babylonian captivity, reflecting the Jewish exile. It began in 1309 and lasted for 68 years until Urban VI returned papacy to Rome. (Adrian Scott Stokes [1854–1935]).

posting of the Archbishop of Canterbury, the monarch was excommunicated and England was placed under a six-year edict which barred all church services. Although John was unconcerned on a spiritual level, he discovered he was vulnerable to the attacks of zealous pro-Rome rulers, in his case Philip of France. John duly made his peace with the Pope; the position of the Church appeared unassailable.

By the 13th century, the clergy were straying from the teachings of Jesus much as the Jews before them had lapsed from the laws of Moses. For centuries it was not unusual to find a bishop with one or more mistresses secreted away, and this was after they were supposed to have taken a vow of celibacy.

Similarly, many lived in style, indulging in rich foods and wines and showing barely a passing interest in society's outcasts who had so inspired Jesus. One priest even observed, "Peasants are coarse, blubbery, gluttonous, rough-skinned, dirty, and their crooked manners are a consequence of their crooked bodies." So much for "Love thy Neighbor."

The political divisions inside the Church remained. The Catholic Church has a history of some 40 antipopes, pretenders to the title, the first being Hippolitus in the 3rd century. Rulers in the Holy Roman Empire frequently nominated antipopes in a bid to control the Vatican as it grew ever stronger and more independent. Last in the series of antipopes were those who sat at Avignon in opposition to the Popes of Rome.

GIVE A POPE A HOME

With the ascendancy of France in the world arena in the Middle Ages, it seemed reasonable to elect French Popes based in France, and from 1309 that is where the Catholic church was focused. The opulence of their palace at Avignon became the subject of worldwide criticism. In a bid to stem the rising tide of opposition, a reforming Italian Pope, Urban VI, was elected who left Avignon for the Vatican in 1378. The choice failed to unify the Church, however, and a body of cardinals elected a second Pope, Clement VII, to sit in France. Further confusion arose when a third Pope declared himself in Prague. It was not until the Council of Constance held between 1414 and 1418 that the issue was resolved. A compromise candidate, Martin V, was invested and made Rome his seat.

THE CRUSADES AND INQUISITION

Between the 11th and 15th centuries, the Catholic Church was associated with two long-running issues which amply illustrated the unacceptable face of Catholicism: the Crusades and the Inquisition.

The Pope sought glorification to boost the flagging support in the Catholic Church, and what better way than in armed struggle against an expansionist faction, the Muslims or "Infidels?" Spiritual strength would no longer suffice. Strong-arm tactics were now deemed essential.

In 1095, the first Crusade was launched by the papacy. On July 15, 1099, Jerusalem fell to papal warriors amid scenes of hideous butchery. Jews died alongside Muslims. It was 90 years before the Muslims took back the territory under the inspiring leadership of Saladin.

The second Crusade (1147–1148) was inconclusive, as was the third (1189–1192), an effort by England, Germany, and France to oust Saladin. The fourth, in 1204, was designed to sack Egypt, but contented itself with Constantinople, still a Christian city but of the Orthodox strain. The pillaging was so outrageous it even earned a rebuke from Pope Innocent III. "It was not heavenly riches upon which your minds were set, but earthly ones. Nothing has been sacred to you. You have violated married women, widows, even nuns. You have despoiled the very sanctuaries of God's Church."

Knights, soldiers, accompanying priests, and the Catholic faith took a share of the booty. Little was gained from the Crusades in terms of power and influence, although much blood was spilled and the enmity between the Christian, Muslim, and Jewish faiths was thoroughly endorsed and thereafter endured.

THE HOLY OFFICE

Then came the Inquisition, or Holy Office, instituted in 1231 by Pope Gregory IX. It was designed to rout the growing number of heretics. These were not people who denied the existence of God but those who questioned the actions of the Pope and the Catholic Church. With corruption, drunkenness, greed, and lascivious behaviour evident in all tiers of the Church hierarchy, people were wavering from the path laid down by the Pope.

At first, secular forces acted as Inquisitors on behalf of the Pope, and soldiers went to

"Kill them all. God will know his own." The Abbot of Citeaux, after being asked who should be spared by the Inquisition in southern France.

work against the Waldensians and the Cathars of southern France who disavowed the authority of the Pope.

But the Holy Roman Empire's forces could not be relied upon to undertake such vital work to the extent envisaged by the Pope. First bishops and later friars from the Dominican and Franciscan orders were detailed to scour Europe for heretics. By 1256 a Papal Bull permitted them to use torture. The friars became the investigators, with juries traditionally made up of priests. Guilt was decided on the word of two witnesses in a system that was vulnerable to corruption. Then the prisoner was handed over

to the secular authorities. The punishment for heresy was to be burnt at the stake.

The paranoia of the Church was infectious. Neighbor denounced neighbor as the Inquisition moved from town to town. Those who instantly confessed to being a heretic and paid the necessary fines or maybe made a pilgrimage were welcomed back to the fold. Those who stood by their denials—and many were presumably good Catholics—were destined to die.

Between the 13th and 16th centuries, the Inquisition won notoriety for its cruelty and needless killing for reasons of excessive piety and devotion in observance of God's wishes.

The villains were zealous friars, men of God who might once have been relied upon for more benevolent conduct.

The Catholic Church has a rich tradition of monasteries initiated by St. Anthony of Egypt (c.251–356), who withdrew into isolation in A.D. 305 to wrestle with temptation. When he emerged he organized the first monastery.

Communities of monks and nuns sprang up across Europe, usually in remote areas. As the excesses of the Church grew more outrageous, so the more devout would seek a monastic life. The ambition of many monks was to reform the double standards of the Church. Some orders, however, fell victim to the same lust for power that crippled the Church. The Dominicans and the Franciscans, whose energies were employed in the Inquisition, lost sight of their humble origins to become the "thought police" of Europe. It is hard to believe that anyone professing a link with the gentle St. Francis of Assisi, who founded the Franciscan order in 1209, could administer the horrors of the Inquisition.

The Pope was decreed infallible. So when Italian scientist Galileo Galilei upheld that the earth moves around the sun, when the Pope had preached the opposite, he found himself in an Inquisitor's court. Polish astronomer Nicolaus Copernicus had formed the same theory in 1543, but kept quiet for fear of papal reprisals. Galileo was twice brought before the Inquisition and banned from discussing planetary movements.

"I want to preach, I want to talk, I want to write, but I do not want to force anyone, for faith needs to be voluntary and free and received without fear."
Martin Luther.

An abuse of power by the Catholic Church was the root cause of the Reformation. This was no dispute about heavenly matters or the nature of God, Jesus, and the Holy Ghost. The issues were earthbound and surrounded the manipulative interpretation of God's will by the Pope.

Martin Luther (1483–1546), a monk, found the sale of indulgences by clergymen, in which sins were forgiven for a financial consideration, a bizarre distortion of Christian

REFORMATION

doctrine. Surely, he argued, man could reach heaven only through his personal faith.

In 1517 Luther produced his 95 Theses, challenging the might of the Papacy, and nailed them to the door of the church at Wittenburg. Luther's aim was to stimulate internal reform, and, as an academic, he enjoyed some initial protection from the wrath of the established Church. However, an full frontal attack on the Pope in his *Appeal to the Christian Nobility of the German Nation* in 1520, was overstepping the mark and led to his excommunication.

Below: Luther depicted at Weinberg with the reformers as the good, and the Catholic Church as the bad wine growers.

It was a sign of the times that, while the out-of-touch Catholic Church was shocked and horrified by Luther's outpourings, his message found a sympathetic hearing among lay people.

In 1521 Luther was summoned to appear before the *diet*, or assembly, at Worms in southwest Germany. If the Church authorities believed Luther would recant, they were disappointed. Not only did he stand by his ideas but he became a rallying point for the people.

The broad support received by Luther was to cause him problems, however. His banner was taken up by the fanatical leader of the peasants' revolt in Germany, Thomas Muntzer (1489–1525). Luther felt unable to condone the ensuing anarchy and lent his support to the Princes and the state Church instead. He was also at odds with Huldreich Zwingli (1484–1531), the radical Swiss church reformer, over whether Christ was really present in the bread broken at Mass, as Luther believed, or whether the ritual of the Last Supper was purely symbolic. Nor was Luther in harmony with Desiderius Erasmus (1466–1536), the Dutch translator of the Greek New Testament and critic of the Catholic Church. Nevertheless, the doctrines that bear his name still exist today.

Luther is remembered not only as a campaigner for religious change, but also as a translator of the Bible and the author of some 42 hymns, some of which were written during the year following his excommunication that he spent in hiding at Wartburg Castle under the protection of the Elector Frederick of Saxony.

In 1534, Luther left the monastery at Wittenberg and a year later he married a former Cistercian nun, Katharina von Bora. They had six children.

JOHN CALVIN

France's great reformer was John Calvin (1509–1564), a law and theology student who began campaigning for Protestantism in the 1530s. During a visit to Geneva in 1536, he met Guillaume Farel (1489–1565), another fervent reformer already exiled from France because of his activities, and together they tried to establish Protestantism in the city. In 1538 both were banished by their opponents. Calvin joined

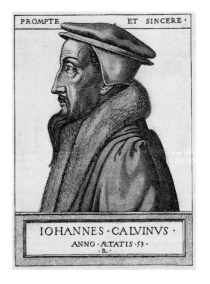

PROMPTE ET SINCERE·

IOHANNES · CALVINVS ·
ANNO · ÆTATIS ·53·
· B ·

Far left: **Martin Luther by Lucas Cranach the Elder (1472–1553).**

Above: **John or Johann Calvin sought to turn Geneva into a model community ruled over by the Protestant Church.**

forces with Martin Bucer (1491–1551), a former Dominican friar, who abandoned his vows in the initial wave of reformation and became adviser to the English king Henry VIII.

Farel won entry back into Geneva and Calvin followed, aiming to make the city a model of Protestantism, with a welfare system and employment controls. He saw Geneva as a new breed of Christian city formed "to nourish and support the exterior service of God." The city would breed decent, virtuous, and charitable citizens.

Calvin shared some of Luther's beliefs, for example, in the authority of the Scriptures and the importance of personal faith. Calvin further believed that some people had been chosen for salvation; these he called "the Elect," while the rest of the population, who were deemed "the Reprobates," would bear the anger of God. He also wanted to see the Church running the state. His most famous works were the *Institutes of the Christian Religion* (1536) which lay down the rules for the Reformed Church. The state churches of Holland and Scotland and some of the non-conformist churches in North America and Germany owe much to Calvinism.

Right: Henry VIII (1491–1547), familiar in this popular portrait by Holbein (1497–1543), shaped the face of religion in Britain to suit his personal ends.

REFORMATION IN ENGLAND

The new Church evolved in England through a different and far less virtuous route than in Europe. Yes, monks and priests were renowned for drinking and womanizing. Yes, the taxes imposed by the Catholic Church in Rome were unpopular. But the birth of the new religious movement was due more to one man's vendetta than any doctrinal debate.

England had always been rather an outpost for the Catholic Church. While the rest of Europe submitted to the Inquisitors, the English kings had refused them entry. Nevertheless, King Henry VIII was happy to embrace the Church and its authority until its interests clashed with his own. Henry was married for almost a quarter of a century to Catherine of Aragon (1485–1536), the widow of his elder brother Arthur. For years he had hoped for a son and

heir, but Catherine gave birth to only one child that lived, a girl called Mary.

"THE KING'S GREAT MATTER"

Henry began a liaison with Anne Boleyn and she became pregnant. Now he was desperate to rid himself of his wife and, with the help of Cardinal Thomas Wolsey (1475–1530), sought an annulment from Rome. Henry's grounds were somewhat doubtful. He questioned the legitimacy of marrying the widow of a dead brother. The Pope wasn't convinced and an annulment was not forthcoming.

Henry's hopes were only realized after his chief adviser, Thomas Cromwell (1485–1540), drew up a series of laws that made the monarch, rather than the Pope, head of the Church in England. First Cromwell curbed the powers of the Church in England, then, when the muscle-flexing did not work in Rome, he all but abolished it. The *"Act of Supremacy"* in 1534 enabled Henry to grant himself a divorce. The triumph against Rome was complete.

Moreover, Cromwell helped to organize the dissolution of the monasteries, reducing many of England's finest buildings to rubble and leaving destitute scores of poor people who had sought food and shelter from them. Cromwell might have wished he had not bothered. When the marriage he negotiated between Henry and Anne of Cleves did not work out he was promptly beheaded.

"The King's Great Matter," as his marital problems were known, just happened to occur as a wave of Protestantism was sweeping Europe and so England followed. It would be wrong to assume that England would still be Catholic if Catherine of Aragon had produced a clutch of sons. After all, from his parish in Leicestershire, reformer John Wyclif (1328 –1384) was one of the first voices of dissent against the Catholic Church, and the Lollards, who followed him, remained active. But because of the King's displeasure, the vestiges of Catholicism were swiftly crushed.

When Henry died, to be succeeded by his 10-year-old son Edward VI, the cause of Protestantism was furthered in 1549 by the first of the *Acts of Uniformity* which introduced the *Book of Common Prayer*, especially formulated for worship by Protestants. Changes were made to strengthen the *Book of Common Prayer* in 1552. However, a year later it was abolished entirely when Edward died, aged 16, to be followed onto the throne by Mary. Now the pendulum swung back. She was a devout Catholic and dispatched nearly 300 people to die at the stake in the name of Catholicism, many times more than had died at the hands of Protestants.

"Bloody Mary" died in 1558 and now it was her half-sister Elizabeth's turn to dictate the faith of the nation. Although she ruled with a spirit of compromise, Elizabeth reestablished Protestantism with a new *"Supremacy Act"* in 1559. The country became obsessed with papist plots, few of which ever materialized.

GUNPOWDER, TREASON AND PLOT

The Gunpowder Plot of 1605 was an attempt by a group of Catholics, led by Robert Catesby, to blow up King James I and the entire English Parliament. Guy Fawkes is the best-known member, who was arrested, horribly tortured, and killed.

In 1678 Titus Oates and Israel Tonge hatched the Popish Plot, laying false allegations about Catholic plans to assassinate King Charles II. More than 35 suspects were executed before the ruse was discovered.

Above: **Mary I, the daughter of Henry VIII by his first wife, was determined to drive her people back into the arms of the Catholic Church.**

METHODISM

The Reformation did not end division within the Church and soon there were many shades of Protestantism—common threads were a deep-rooted opposition to Catholicism and a simplicity of faith, although each faction had its own characteristics.

Above: **John Wesley was a student at Oxford and later a Fellow of Lincoln College and devoted much time to religious debate.**

The Methodists were among the most significant of the dissident groups and were born out of the efforts of John Wesley (1703–1791). He was the 13th of 19 children of an Anglican priest and his wife. A brilliant student, he went to Oxford University where, with his younger brother Charles (1707–1788), he joined a religious society. A characteristic of this puritanical student society was its well-ordered lifestyle which allowed time for prayer, Bible study, and goodwill visits and it was soon laughingly branded "Methodist."

This was not the start of the new church, however, for the group broke up acrimoniously and in 1735 the Wesley brothers, who had both been ordained, decided to become missionaries in Georgia in the United States. This

Left: **Methodist chapels, like this one at Heptonstall in West Yorkshire, England, are traditionally simplistic both inside and out.**

venture was not a success, but on the way back the Wesleys had their first meeting with members of the Moravian church, an offshoot of the Lutherans established in 1722 by Count Nikolaus von Zinzendorf. The creed of the Moravian faith was faith, love, and repentance.

On May 27, 1738, while listening to a sermon written by Luther, Wesley experienced enlightenment. The single most important fact in life was faith, Wesley decided, and all else followed. He organized a series of meetings at which people were equally filled with new-found enthusiasm for their faith. The impromptu responses of the congregations in shouting or prostrating themselves was out of line with Anglican practice and, although it was not Wesley's intention to initiate a division, the Methodists (as they became known later) split from the main Anglican church.

A tireless writer, John Wesley traveled Britain on horseback to preach. Charles is remembered as a prolific writer of hymns.

Today Methodist churches are distinguished by their functional decor. There are rows of benches (Methodists remain seated to pray), an organ to provide music, which is a key part of the worship, and often schoolrooms are incorporated. Women have been permitted to become ministers since 1973.

THE QUAKERS

English Methodism came in the wake of the Quakers, or Society of Friends, founded by George Fox (1624–1691). Fox was a Puritan by upbringing, a strictly moral Christian movement which held sway in England between 1649 and 1660. Puritans were rabidly anti-Catholic and so fervently in favor of Christian simplicity that they would not countenance any of the Orthodox liturgy.

Fox himself was opposed to state control of the Church. In 1646 he experienced a personal revelation and afterward preached a gospel of love. He called his followers the Society of Friends because he urged them to be friends of Christ. Persecution of the Quakers was so intense that in 1682 William Penn led a group to America, and thus founded Pennsylvania.

Quakers are still known today as resolute pacifists, while being remembered as tireless workers for the emancipation of slaves and prison reform. At Quaker meetings there is silence until someone is moved by the "inner light" to speak. There is no hierarchy, sacraments, or oath-taking.

In 1827, the Plymouth Brethren appeared, an evangelical Protestant movement with its roots in Puritanism. Like the Puritans, the Brethren frowned on many worldly pleasures, including alcohol and gambling, as well as any form of religious imagery. The Brethren are divided into closed and open groups. Those in the former have no contact with people outside the church, even if they are family members.

THE SALVATION ARMY

Fifty years later, the Salvation Army was founded in London, England, by William Booth (1829–1929). Booth began his new movement in response to the reluctance of the established denominations to accept converts he had made in the inner-city slums. He ran the Salvation Army on military lines with associated ranks. Highly moral, the "Sally Army," as it is fondly known, frowns on alcohol and smoking. It is perhaps best known for the brass bands that play at services, its newspaper *War Cry,* and the successful missing persons bureau it runs.

Above: **William Bramwell Booth ran the Salvation Army along military lines and expected absolute obedience from his flock.**

When it became clear that synagogues and temples were no longer appropriate places for the devotees of Jesus Christ to worship, St. Paul hit upon the notion of churches.

These were, however, a luxury not afforded to the earliest Christians as they endured the persecution of Roman emperors. Christianity was an underground movement and they worshipped, quite literally, below ground in the catacombs that threaded beneath northeast and southern Rome. The catacombs used by the Christians are still distinguishable from those used by Jews and Romans by the frescoes on the walls, which feature scenes of the Last Supper and Jesus's miracles.

Sites of other early churches have been erased by time, probably because there was little to set them apart from other non-specific buildings of the era. The oldest church in Britain, in a Roman villa in Lullingstone in Kent, was only recognized for what it was by the Christian symbols which had been preserved on the walls. Otherwise it would have appeared like any other room. However, churches soon adopted a regular design, one that they have kept to this day.

CHURCHES AND CATHEDRALS

Right: Notre-Dame de Paris is the famous Gothic cathedral built between 1163 and 1345 on the Ile de la Cité to replace two previous churches. Badly damaged during the French Revolution of 1789, it has since been restored.

Basically it comprises a rectangle with a semi-circle or polygon on its eastern end, the apse. You might find the pulpit, altar, door, and font placed similarly in many houses of worship. The joy of churches and cathedrals, however, is that no two are the same. Building styles include Saxon, Norman, Gothic, Baroque, and Gothic revival, while the internal features are many and varied.

DICTIONARY OF THE CHURCH
Almonry: where help was given to the poor and sick.

Altar: communion table and focal point, also known as a *mensa*. The first were made of wood and were known as "Christ's Board," but after 1076 they were consecrated only if they were made of stone. The finest were some 10 feet long and a ton in weight. Trends changed and in Elizabethan times the fashion in England was once more for wood.

Ambulatory: passage behind high altar, leading from one side of the church to the other.

Anchorite cell: lean-to built on the side of a parish church for hermits in the Middle Ages. Once the devout anchorite had entered, the door was sealed. The inmate had one window into the church to view services and one hatch on an outside wall through which food and water were passed. Once inside, an anchorite never left the cell alive.

Aumbry: closet for the cups and plates used in the Eucharist.

Baptistery: housing for the font. Most fonts are covered after a law was passed in the 13th century to prevent the theft of holy water.

Gargoyle: carved water spout which relieves the roof of rainwater without damaging the church walls.

Lady Chapel: a chapel dedicated to the Virgin Mary.

Lectern: reading desk, often in the form of a spread eagle.

Misericord: ledges on the edges of tip-up seats which gave support to elderly clergy when they were compelled to stand during long services.

Nave: main area for congregation.

Pews: seating appeared in churches in the middle of the 13th century which hitherto had

"Where two or three are gathered together in my name I am present in their midst." *Matthew 18:20*

"1704 Dec 6th was buried the stinking residue of William Gwylliams." Parish record at Elkstone, Gloucestershire, England.

Belfry: bell housing.

Bells: a principal reason for building church towers, the bells within are thought to have been associated with Christian worship since the 5th century.

Buttress: brick or masonry support.

Carrel: recessed seat used by monks.

Cathedral: principal church of the diocese, from the Greek word *cathedra*, a seat.

Chancel: the eastern end of the church where the main altar is sited.

Chantry: small chapel where once priests, working on commission, would chant masses for the souls of wealthy families. The practice was forbidden by an Act in 1529.

Chapter house: meeting room for deans and canons who form the chapter of a cathedral.

Clerestory: upper level of church wall; its windows light the center of the building.

been empty. From the 15th century the bench ends were often elaborately carved.

Piscina: small basin near the altar used for washing sacramental vessels.

Pulpit: platform for preacher, sometimes raised so he can address upper platforms.

Sacristy: room where sacred vessels are kept.

Sanctuary: area at the eastern end of the church containing the altar.

Sedilia: seats for the clergy built into the south wall of the chancel, frequently in threes and at various heights.

Stained glass windows: in the 12th century, glass mosaics held by strips of lead replaced the oiled linen of Saxon times. Soon decorative windows were used to venerate saints or featured heraldry.

Vestry: room adjoining the church used by clergy and choir for changing.

CHRISTIAN FESTIVALS

Advent	November/December
Christmas	December 25
Lent	40 days before Easter
Easter	March/April
Ascension Day	Thursday after fourth Sunday after Easter
Pentecost or Whitsuntide	Seven Sundays after Easter
Trinity Sunday	Sunday after Pentecost

Advent starts the Christian year, a reminder of the coming of Christ. In the West, Advent begins four Sundays before Christmas, while the Eastern Orthodox church marks the same period with a 40-day-long period of penitence. Advent was not introduced into the Church calendar until the 6th century.

CHRISTMAS SYMBOLISM

Critics of Christianity take pleasure in pointing out that no-one knows when Jesus was born and that December 25 was once an important pagan celebration. There is little doubt that the date which was once precious to worshippers of Mithras, the sun god, was hijacked by early Christians as part of missionary conversion tactics. None of this detracts from the special meaning that the celebration holds for Christians. It symbolizes how God made a gift of his only son to the world and how that son, Jesus, brought with him light and love.

By A.D. 336, Christmas was celebrated on December 25. The Christmas tree, holly, and ivy, symbols of Christmas, are all linked strongly to the pagan midwinter festivities when the evergreen foliage bore the significance of survival in the cold, dark winter. Mistletoe—a symbol of the Druids who indulged in human sacrifice—was never welcomed in the same way in churches simply because of this association.

St. Francis of Assisi introduced the use of a crib in connection with the Christ Child in 1223 and it has been a regular feature ever since. Midnight Mass was a custom which originally occurred at Easter but has become a part of Christmas instead.

Christmas is now also a secular celebration and it is this aspect which brings forth a great feast. These days a turkey is normally served whereas in the past in Europe it might have been a goose or even a swan.

POST-CHRISTMAS CELEBRATIONS

Hot on the heels of Christmas comes the Feast of the Holy Innocents, on December 28, commemorating the slaughter of all infant males in Bethlehem by the jealous Herod. In Christianity the suffering of the children is seen as a precursor to the torment of Christ.

The cycle of Christmas festivals ends with Epiphany on January 6 which once marked the baptism of Jesus by John the Baptist, or his first miracle at Cana, but now commemorates the adoration of the Magi.

Lent, a period of abstinence, begins on Ash Wednesday and lasts for 40 days. It follows Shrove Tuesday. Traditionally pancakes were made on this day to rid the house of fat before the fasting began. Ash Wednesday derived its name from the ancient practice of marking the foreheads of worshippers with a smudge of ashes to perpetuate humility.

Left: Traditional Whit Sunday celebrations with participants clad in white are captured on canvas in 1888 by Edouard Durand.

Below: Baptism is not the preserve of infants. Baptists, like these from Eastbourne, England, demand adults make this commitment.

Lent is the time in which Christians reflect and pay penance, rejecting material luxuries in favor of spiritual concerns. Once it was strongly associated with religious teaching. The final week of Lent is holy week, leading up to the crucifixion and subsequent resurrection of Christ.

The Day of Ascension, 40 days after Easter Sunday, falls on a Thursday. It marks the departure of Jesus from earth to heaven—apparently on a cloud—after he spoke to his disciples on the Mount of Olives for the last time and urged them to preach the gospel. Islam also has its Ascension Day, but it refers to Muhammad's journey in the company of Gabriel to meet God.

Whitsuntide or Pentecost occurs 50 days after Easter, to commemorate when the Apostles were filled with the Holy Spirit. In Luke's Gospel, Jesus explained it to the disciples like this: "I am sending upon you my Father's promised gift; so stay here in this city until you are armed with the power from above."

By ancient tradition, those baptized at Easter would wear the same white or "whit" garment until Pentecost or Whit Sunday.

CHAPTER EIGHT

ISLAM

A relative newcomer, Islam is one of the success stories of the world's religions. It began in a dusty corner of Arabia a mere few centuries ago—which makes it the most modern of the great faiths—through the efforts of one man, Muhammad. He broadcast the divine messages he received from God to all those who would listen, at first only a few, and, in the best tradition of prophets, he was driven out of his home town and ridiculed. But his persistence and profound faith were ultimately rewarded when his band of followers multiplied and he turned the pagan face of Mecca toward God. Today there are millions of Muslims. The religion is dominant in the countries of North Africa, the Middle East, Western Asia, and Indonesia.

Although Muslims pray to Allah, this is in fact the same God worshipped by Christians and Jews by a different name. Allah is an Arabic term comprising two words: *Al* which means "the" and *Illah* which means "God." To Muslims, the name Allah is preferable to that of God because it appears in their holy book, the *Qur'an*, it has no male or female gender, and it cannot be pluralized in the same way that "God" can become "gods." The change of name from God is just one of many ways in which Islam is widely misunderstood in the West. The kernel of distrust was planted centuries ago by the Crusaders and after the cruel violence between Muslims and Christians the tolerance preached by both Muhammad and

Muhammad, the Prophet, known variously as "Beloved of God" and "Joy of Creation," is central to the Islamic faith. Despite their devout reverence and respect for him, Muslims do not worship Muhammad. To do so would mean committing one of the greatest sins of Islam—elevating someone on a par with God. Muhammad was the instigator of the Muslim religion, but he acted at the behest of God and was a servant of God.

MUHAMMAD

Above: **The archangel appears to Muhammad and reveals to him heavenly truths which later appear in the** *Qur'an.*

A SACRED ORPHAN

Muhammad was born in about A.D. 570 in Mecca (or Makkah), a gem of a city whose richness contrasts dramatically with the barren hills of western Saudi Arabia which embrace it. In religious terms, Mecca was already an important site. Its chief attraction was the Kaaba, a monument originally built by Abraham. By the time of Muhammad's birth, the Kaaba was devoted to numerous deities and was strewn with idols. The city flourished as a key staging post for the merchants who plied their trade between Southern Arabia and the Mediterranean.

Muhammad's father, Abdullah, had died before he was born and he was orphaned at the age of six when his mother, Amina, died. Care of the child passed to his blind grandfather who died just two years later. He became the ward of an uncle, Abu Talib, and under his guardianship Muhammad forged a career in

trade. Some Muslims insist he was entirely uneducated, but, even if he had no formal education, Muhammad certainly encountered the Christian, Jewish, and Pagan faiths which prevailed among the travelers he met. Through his work he met a rich widow, Khadija, some 15 years his senior and at her suggestion they wed. Khadija bore him six or seven children, but his three sons died in infancy.

From his early years it seems Muhammad was marked out for greatness. During her pregnancy, his mother heard angelic voices proclaiming the arrival of a prophet. It is claimed two angels visited him when he was an infant to rub away a black clot of sin from his heart using snow drawn from a golden basin. On his back there was a patch of skin surrounded by hair—deemed by many to be a mark of greatness. Even a Christian monk foretold the future role of 12-year-old Muhammad.

THE NIGHT OF DESTINY

By the age of 40, Muhammad was spending more and more time praying and meditating in the isolation of the mountains. On Mount Hira, the angel Gabriel appeared to him while

Left: Bedouins were early converts to Islam.
Below: Muhammad and his men poised to attack Mecca.

Jesus and Mary, untouched. This time, when he urged the people to turn to God, Muhammed found sympathetic listeners. He returned to Yathrib, renamed Medina "city of the prophet," to his family. By now Khadija had died and he had taken other wives—there were ten in total—and two concubines, although his dream of having a son was never fulfilled.

Despite a natural tolerance of other religions, Muhammad felt bound to expel or exterminate the colonies of Jews who so vehemently denied his message. Muhammad died of intestinal problems in A.D. 632.

he slept. At last Muhammad knew he had been appointed as a special messenger and through him God's word would be spread on earth. From that moment, the "Night of Power" or "Night of Destiny," Muhammad had regular revelations, which were later to become assembled as the *Qur'an* or Koran.

On receiving a message, Muhammad would fall into a trance, the onset of which he could not control. He would go silent and his face would glow and perspire, even on cold days. Some reported a gentle humming sound emanating from his face. As the intensity of the trance subsided, he would recite verses in a style completely alien to his own. Afterward, even Muhammad was surprised by the content of the verses which came from his lips.

Muhammad preached his new religion, urging the Meccans to reject idolatry and worship only one God. However, he discovered his enthusiasm was not shared; such was the hostility of fellow Meccans that he and his faithful few had to flee to Yathrib in 622, which later became Year 1 of the Muslim calendar. From Yathrib he consolidated his position and incited his army of 300 into conflict, triumphing over one three times its size. His campaign gained momentum until by 630 he marched victoriously into Mecca. His first act was to smash the images of pagan gods which decorated the Kaaba, leaving just one picture, of

QUR'AN

Centuries after the death of Muhammad, his words continue to echo in the ears of every Muslim. The revelations he uttered in elegant Arabic are still available to all, thanks to the *Qur'an*, or "recitation." It is, say followers, God's last word to mankind.

THE WORD OF GOD

According to Muhammad, the revelations that eventually comprised the *Qur'an* were taken from a heavenly book containing God's wisdom. All of the holy books, including the Gospel of Jesus and the Jewish *Torah*, were taken from this divine charter, called the *Mother of the Book*. God decided to impart still more so that the Arabs would be addressed in their own language and would hear the undiluted word of God.

At first the words of the Prophet were written on parchment or in clay by attendant scribes (the art of papermaking had not yet been brought to Arabia). Given the era and the difficulties of transporting the text, people generally chose to learn the sacred doctrines by heart.

One of Muhammad's secretaries, Zayd ibn Thabit, began gathering the verses of the *Qur'an* soon after the Prophet's death. He discovered the words inscribed on leather, stones, palm leaves, and even on the shoulder-blades of camels. He interviewed Muhammad's closest associates to find out more and also placed some kind of order on the verses where none previously existed.

The third Caliph, or successor to Muhammad, decided to avoid potential controversy over the content of the *Qur'an* by creating an official and authentic version. The work of Thabit formed its basis, all other versions were destroyed, and it has never since been altered or modified. Accordingly the *Qur'an* is instantly recognizable, at least to Muslims, today. Nothing has since been changed and the 6,666 verses, still in Arabic, are how Muhammad himself would remember them.

Below: **Although intricately decorated, mosques, like this one in Dubai, bear no images of God, Muhammad or the saints.**

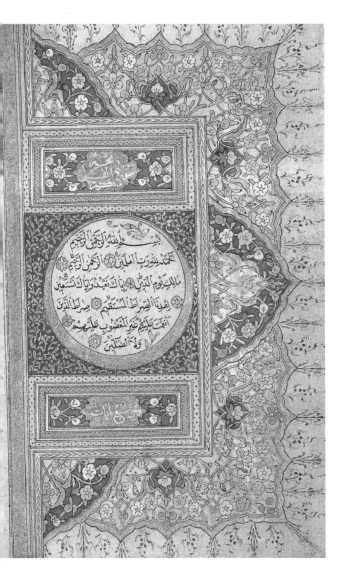

Muslims argue that the indisputable *Qur'an* is more authoritative than the Bible, as the latter was written by numerous people years after the death of Christ. The sacred *Qur'an* is cherished by Muslims.

ASSOCIATED SUPERSTITION

A Muslim would never leave the *Qur'an* on the floor or, indeed, anywhere that it could become soiled. As a mark of their devotion to Islam Muslims might memorize the entire book, even if it is in a different language from their own, to recite it during the festival of Ramadam. Devout Muslims write each verse out by hand to make a beautifully illuminated personal copy. Children, particularly boys, are sent to learn about the *Qur'an*.

The insistence by Muslim scholars that the *Qur'an* should stay in its original language is not just dogmatic, for the verses are in a kind of attractively rhyming prose which would be lost in translation. Translations have, of course, been made, but these usually bear titles which identify them as being different from the original *Qur'an*. Translations might also reverse the order of the chapters as the longest chapters appear first in the *Qur'an*—Chapter 2 has 286 verses—and the number diminishes as the book proceeds, so that Chapter 110 only has three verses. Another feature of translations is that they number the 114 chapters (or *suras*) although in the original Arabic they have names, including *Abraham*, the *Cow* and the *Unity*.

There are also books which seek to explain the mystique of the holy book. The *Qur'an* is not encyclopedic in detail and it presumes some knowledge of the time-honored tales it includes. Some of the stories reflect those in the Bible—Jesus is reverently referred to, although his crucifixion is ignored. Qur'anic references are sometimes oblique, allegoric, and only occasionally forthright. An explanatory tome is called a *tafsir* and the best known is by the author al-Tabari who died in A.D. 923.

Every chapter in the *Qur'an* except one begins, "In the name of God, the Merciful, the Compassionate."

Each day dutiful Muslims will frequently quote the opening prayer:

"In the Name of God, the Merciful,
the Compassionate.
Praise be to God, the Lord of the worlds,
The Merciful, the Compassionate.
King on the Day of Judgment.
Thee do we serve and on thee do we call for help.
Guide us on the straight path,
The path of those to whom thou hast been gracious,
Not of those upon whom anger falls, or those who
go astray."

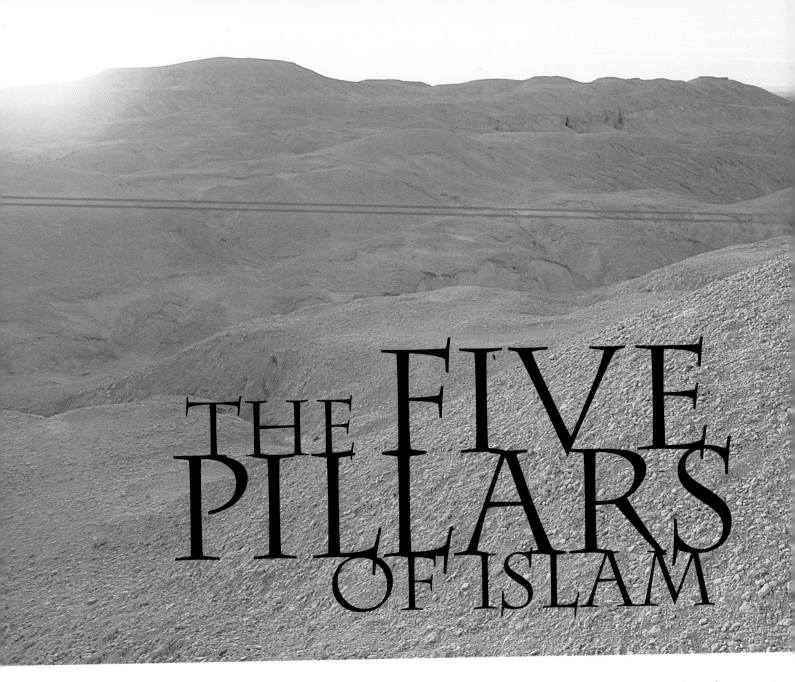

THE FIVE PILLARS OF ISLAM

In Islam there are five golden rules. If the faith is seen in terms of a great building, then these rules are the pillars which hold it up. Every Muslim knows he must observe his obligations to God or risk the pillars crumbling, undermining the very foundations of the religion.

1. SHAHADAH

The principal pillar is the confession of faith: that there is only one God and that Muhammad is his final prophet. The relevant lines of the *Qur'an* which affirm this belief are repeated at the start and end of the five-times-daily prayers and again during periods of meditation. The *shahadah* compels Muslims to declare their unswerving faith in the *Qur'an*, in angels, and the Last Day. It is a daily reminder that a belief in false gods is one of the cardinal sins of Islam.

2. SALAT

Utmost importance is given to the frequency of prayer. It was Muhammad himself who decreed that prayers should be said five times every day. This gives every Muslim a guaranteed time of tranquillity to reflect on the faith. When a Muslim bows down facing Mecca, he does so in the knowledge that millions are doing just the same around the globe and this repetition is supremely comforting.

body before a further *sujud*. This cycle may be repeated a number of times, depending on the length of prayers. It ends with the *shahadad*, the greeting of *salaam* (peace be with you) to fellow worshippers.

3. ZAKAT

The third pillar concerns the giving of alms, or *zakat*. This is no charitable whim by Muslims, but an humanitarian tax. The word *zakat* translates to "purification" and "growth." It helps to link all members of the community for, as Muhammad put it, "if one suffers then all others rally in response."

Its aims are mutually beneficial. The giver is purged of selfishness and atones for sin, while the recipient vanquishes the powerful emotion of envy. For each individual or family the amount of *zakat* varies, but it is approximately two and one-half percent of net wealth.

This is not merely a penalty for the rich, but for all citizens of means. Nor is it a source of pride or personal glorification, for *zakat* is expected of people rather than being a noble choice. *Zakat* gives the poor a stake in the riches of the wealthy. Muhammad felt that *zakat* greatly contributed toward a just and balanced society.

The Prophet did not expect his people to impoverish themselves, but to give proportionately to their wealth. Those who could not give materially were expected to think and act charitably. Islamic wisdom warns of dire consequences in the hereafter for those who turn their backs on this obligation.

An extension of *zakat* is *sadaqa*, an act of charity above that which is required. It would be usual to keep such donations secret. Once again God would know if the underlying motives were genuine or inspired only by arrogance, Muhammad warned.

Initially, prayers were said facing Jerusalem. However, in A.D. 624 the Prophet changed the direction to Mecca, specifically to the religiously significant Kaaba.

Body and mind are united in the discipline of prayer. There are 13 essentials, known as *arkan*, to be observed. The formula for prayer is the same for Muslims everywhere, another binding thread.

To begin, the worshipper stands facing Mecca and, at the second call to prayer, he recites the opening *sura* of the *Qur'an*. After further recitation, he bows deeply, with hands on his knees. Returning to the standing position, he clasps his hands to the side of his face while he prays again, before he undertakes a *sujud*, that is, prostration. He raises his upper

Above: **The Gate of God in Damascus—reputedly the world's oldest city—becomes a focus of expectation at sunset during Ramadam.**

Left: **The end of Ramadam has always been a time of celebration, as this 13th-century impression reveals.**

4. SAWM

To some, the fourth pillar of Islam, a month-long daytime fast, seems harsh or even cruel. To the devout Muslim *sawm*, as the fast is known, is far from it. Although the annual ritual is tough on the stomach, it is spiritually rewarding as a selfless act of union with God.

Sawm is not just for the ascetically-minded; every adult Muslim, male or female, is expected to undertake the fast. Even children are encouraged to experience some form of self-denial, although they are spared the rigors of *sawm*. The only other exceptions are made for nursing mothers, menstruating women, the severely ill, or travelers. If they cannot undertake the abstention which occurs during the Muslim calendar month of Ramadan, then Muslims are obliged to feed a needy person for every day missed or to fast as soon as possible afterward.

Sawm has been a feature of Muslim life since 623, Year 2 of the Muslim calendar, when Muhammad called for a 24-hour fast to mark the anniversary of the flight from Mecca to Medina. This was called the *ashura*. The following year the date assumed even greater importance as it coincided with Muhammad's victory at the battle of Badr, when he defeated the Meccans against overwhelming odds. Later still on this date, the first tract of the *Qur'an* was revealed to the Prophet during Ramadam.

Although the schedule for the holy month is demanding, it is not intended to be one of relentless deprivation. Certainly all food, drink, tobacco, and sexual contact are prohibited during the day. Self-restraint is also called for in social behavior, while evil or hurtful words and actions are against the spirit of *sawm*. Before Ramadam commences, there is *Laila Al-Bar'h*, the "Night of Forgiveness," when old arguments are set aside and wounds are healed. It is with this healthy frame of mind that Ramadam begins.

After sundown, however, the fast is broken with a special meal, *iftar*, often taken with friends or relatives in a joyful rather than somber mood. Eating and drinking can take place until the first rays of morning light. The *Qur'an* dictates that the fast resumes when it is possible to distinguish between a white thread and a black one by natural light.

The benefits to Muslims are clear. The lessons to be learned through abstention are those of patience, will-power, self-discipline, moderation, and communal unity. There is an extra dimension added, too, to the relationship forged between those on earth and God above. It offers a timely reminder that the poor feel those same pangs of hunger every day of the year, not just during a select few.

Unlike the Western solar calendar, Muslim dates are based on lunar cycles and their year is therefore 11 days shorter. This means that Ramadam, the ninth month of the Islamic calendar, moves forward by nearly two weeks every year. Muslims will therefore experience fasting throughout the seasons as the years progress. The acid test of their commitment must surely come in refusing drink during the searingly hot summer sun of Middle Eastern Islamic countries. It is permitted to wet the lips or rinse the inside of a dry mouth, but to gargle would be going too far and would be considered a breaking of the fast. Similarly, a cooling body spray is allowed during *sawm* and, thankfully, so is air conditioning.

Traditionally, Muslims clean their teeth with a *siwak*, a twig from a certain kind of tree, during Ramadam.

As the moon wanes, Ramadam ends with a collective morning prayer followed by four days of celebration known as *eid al-fitr*, the feast of the "Breaking of the Fast." It is a time for family parties and vacations, and children are given presents.

5. HAJJ

As one of hundreds worshipping God at the same time in the same place, *hajj* is a profoundly affecting experience. As one of millions, the result is nothing less than sensational. Being shoulder to shoulder, soul to soul, heart to heart with people as far as the eye can see—and many more still that are in the vicinity but completely out of sight—is an ecstatic experience. For Muslims, it is a life-long ambition.

The fifth and final pillar of Islam concerns the *hajj*, or pilgrimage, to Mecca which Muslims are urged to make at least once in a lifetime. The trek is made during the Islamic

Right: **Sacrifice remains a potent symbol among superstitious Muslims. This Egyptian uses sheep's blood to mark the walls of his home, warding off illness and harvest disasters.**

month of *Dhuil-Hijja*, the 12th in the calendar. The word *hajj* means "visit to the revered place" and the pilgrimage is to pay homage not only to Muhammad but also to Abraham. In Islamic philosophy, he was one of the earliest in a line of God's prophets on earth which ended with Muhammad.

In fact, the legend associated with Mecca extends to the very beginning of Biblical times. It is said that Adam, expelled from Paradise, came to the site of the city to build a temple in praise of God. Using stones from Mount Sinai, the Mount of Olives, and Mount Lebanon, Adam created the first Kaaba and encrusted it with gems. Unfortunately, its fate was not a happy one. It was covered by flood waters at the time of Noah and its finery was reduced to a nondescript hill by the time the region again became a desert.

Abraham came here with his maidservant Hagar and their son Ishmael. He abandoned them to the will of God, aware that their meager food rations and water supply were grossly inadequate for survival. Hagar made desperate attempts to seek water, running between Mount Marwa and the hill of Safa seven times. Finally she saw an angel who asked her why she was weeping. "I thirst," she sobbed. At that the angel touched the ground with a wing tip and up bubbled a fresh spring that was christened Zamzam. Hagar and Ishmael prospered at the site and finally Abraham returned to rebuild the Kaaba on the site of Adam's original monument. In it he incorporated a sacred stone. It is reputed to have been the heavenly symbol of man's soul and was luminous white. The stone was eventually blackened by man's sins. It exists today, having since been identified as a piece of meteorite. The Kaaba is a striking black box of a building and remains key to the complex ritual of the *hajj*.

Newcomers spend the first week at Mecca becoming acquainted with the strict routine of pilgrimage prayers with the help of an army of guides. Once they are within six miles of Mecca, the worshippers may not

"In the Name of God, the Merciful, the Compassionate.
Say: I take refuge with the Lord of men,
The King of men, the God of men,
From the evil of the whispering, the lurking,
Which whispers in the hearts of men,
From among spirits and men."
Last chapter of the *Qur'an*, repeated in daily prayers.

aim is to touch the black stone, but most must be content with saluting it from afar.

To enforce the message during the *hajj* that all men are equal in the sight of God, pilgrims don a white robe, an *ezar*, worn with a pocketed belt and a pair of sandals. Protective headgear for men is expressly forbidden. Although they wear ordinary clothes, women are completely covered except for their face and hands. Drawn from Islamic nations around the world, pilgrims at the *hajj* become one enormous, highly focused, and ultimately spiritually fulfilled family.

However, the *hajj* has had an unhappy history of fatalities. In 1997, several hundred Muslims died and thousands more were injured when a fire swept through 70,000 tents pitched close together in a 10 square mile area. An estimated 270 pilgrims died in 1994 when crowds surged forward uncontrollably. In 1990, overcrowding in a tunnel at Mina claimed the lives of at least 1,420 and three years previously 400 Iranians died in clashes with Saudi security forces.

Below: **The sacred black stone at the Kaaba in Mecca was once pure white, according to legend, until it was stained by man's sin.**

shave or cut their hair or nails until the end of the ceremony.

The official opening of the *hajj* takes place on the seventh day of the month. A day later the pilgrims make their way to the village of Mina, five miles away. At sunrise on day nine they go to Arafat for a sermon which lasts for much of the afternoon. The next assembly point is the Valley of Muzdalifa and the aim is to arrive there in time for evening prayers. Here they gather stones for the ceremony at Mina the following day in which a pillar, representing the devil, is showered with pebbles. Obviously some personal danger is entailed here for, given that two million people may be taking part, each launching seven rocks, few of the stones reach their intended target and most of them fall on the heads and bodies of fellow pilgrims.

There follows a feast of sacrifice. With the large number of animals being sacrificed at the *hajj*, the authorities have established a meat packing plant nearby to enable safe distribution of spare supplies to the poor. The pilgrims then shave, wash, and cut their hair and return to Mecca to circle the Kaaba seven times. Their

King Fahd of Saudi Arabia is the Custodian of the Two Holy Mosques and, as such, is ultimately responsible for the organization of the *hajj*. The Saudi government has a ministry of *hajj* affairs and in 1997 spent nearly £65 million on a fleet of 12,000 buses for pilgrims.

MOSQUES

A mosque is usually thought to be the equivalent of a Christian church, that is, the venue for worship. In fact, to Muslims the whole world is a mosque, a suitable place for prayer. And prayers can be carried out in company or alone. All that is needed is a small area of clean ground, which is why a prayer mat is used.

As Muslims pray five times a day—at dawn, midday, late afternoon, evening, and last thing at night—it would be impractical to perform all of their devotions in the confines of one particular building.

Nonetheless, a mosque remains central to the life of a Muslim community as a meeting place, somewhere to study the *Qur'an* and, of course, for communal prayer.

The towers and domes of a mosque are a familiar and dramatic feature breaking the skyline of Muslim villages, towns, and cities. Istanbul's Blue Mosque is probably the most familiar in the West while the Great Mosque at Mecca—open to Muslims only—is the most sacred.

THE CALL TO PRAYER

A local crier, or *muezzin*, calls from the top of towers or *minarets* at dawn each day. "God is most great, I bear witness that there is no God but God. I bear witness that Muhammad is the Messenger of God. Come to prayer. Prayer is better than sleep."

His chants will ring evocatively through the streets and houses a further four times during the day. Technology has intervened and sometimes it is a tape-recorded cry that brings the faithful to prayer.

WORSHIP WITHIN THE MOSQUE

At least once a day, the ritual of prayer begins with thorough washing of the hands, face, head, legs, and feet. At the mosque, a fountain or *fauwara* is provided at its perimeter. With bare feet, the worshipper enters the prayer hall, or *zulla*, beneath the dome.

Floors and ceilings might well be covered with intricate patterned tiles, the decorations often ornately drawn out of words or letters in the *Qur'an*. There is little else to catch the eye, however. Pictures and statues are forbidden as being images which may detract from the worship of God. There is no furniture, apart from the reading desk, or *minbar*. The floor is covered with mats which are used for prayer, but there are no chairs. On the wall there is the *mihrab*, a decorative niche which indicates the direction of Mecca.

With their bodies facing Mecca and their souls before God, the worshippers pray, uttering verses from the *Qur'an*. The word "mosque" means "place of prostration."

Away from the *zulla* is a screened area reserved for women. While integration during worship between men and women is accelerating in some countries, it is still considered unorthodox to have women praying alongside men at the mosque.

Adult males traditionally gather at the mosque on Fridays to hear a sermon from the *imam*, or religious leader, in a tradition begun by Muhammad at Medina.

SUFISM

Like other religions, Islam has a mystic thread which runs alongside its mainstream theology. Sufism has been at times exulted and sometimes persecuted by Muslims for, although Sufis look to the *Qur'an* for divine inspiration, they also threaten the monotheism which Islam holds so dear.

The term Sufi derives from the Arabic word *suf*, meaning wool, as early Sufis wore plain woollen garments as part of their denial of worldly comforts. They are the equivalent of, and perhaps modeled themselves upon, the early Christian monks and hermits which Arab forces encountered in their forays in the 9th and 10th centuries.

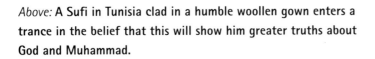

Above: A Sufi in Tunisia clad in a humble woollen gown enters a trance in the belief that this will show him greater truths about God and Muhammad.

THE SAINTS

Questing for unity with God, the Sufis seek hidden and higher truths in Muhammad's revelations. Sufis believe in a network of saints, or *walis*, who pass down the secret knowledge which will set them on a path to God. The saints are discreet. Although they can perform miracles, these men are instructed to keep their talents to themselves during their time on earth.

Sufi worshippers are known as *fakirs*. They will attach themselves to a saint for tuition and guidance, usually as part of a brotherhood.

When a Sufi graduates from pupil to teacher, he is dispatched like a missionary to a distant outpost to spread the word. The most suitable and talented of the pupils is picked by the saint as his *khalifah*, or successor.

MUSICAL MEDITATION

One of the most outstanding differences between Sufi contemplation and Muslim worship is the role of music. Muslims have traditionally distrusted instruments, believing wind instruments and strings to be associated with the devil. Sufis, however, depend on music and sometimes poetry to achieve the necessary state of mind to seek God. A rhythmic drum beat may also promote a trance, a technique used by the practitioners of voodoo. The most famous example of Sufi music is that of the Whirling Dervishes, an Order founded in the 13th century, which was famed for its frenetic dances to fast music.

Once in motion the Sufis chant the *dhikr*, a repetition of God's name and sacred texts from the *Qur'an*. To assist they might also use prayer beads similar to the Catholic rosary.

The aim is to induce self-hypnosis or a state of consciousness in which the Sufi can explore the paths to God.

Muhammad is inspirational to the Sufis, not least because of the celebrated Night Ride or *miraj*. On a flying white mule and in the company of the angel Gabriel, Muhammad went to the Temple of Solomon in Jerusalem, through to the Gates of Heaven and beyond, until he finally came into the presence of God. Devout Muslims believe the Prophet undertook the journey body and soul, while Sufis see the journey as an inner, spiritual ascension.

THE HISTORY OF SUFISM

Sufism is generally categorized into three periods: the classical, medieval, and modern. Prominent among the classical Sufis is Husayn ibn Mansur al-Hallaj, who was crucified for heresy in A.D. 922, after declaring, "I am the truth."

Thereafter, Sufis learned to mask in complex poetry any statements that might be deemed to challenge the "one God" belief, so that only the enlightened could unravel them.

During the Middle Ages, Abu Hamid al-Ghazzali (1059-1111) withdrew from his job and family in search of God. His writings helped to combine the heretical aspects of Sufism with orthodox Islam.

Numerically Sufism reached its peak in the modern age, between about 1550 and 1800. The Sufis actively fought to rid Muslim countries of European colonialists and branched out into all aspects of life. Today Sufism is often practiced covertly in Muslim countries, while in India and the West it commands a faithful following.

Nothing comes between man and God in Islam. Although there are *imams*, or religious leaders, who might be likened to priests, there is no equivalent to the archdeacons, bishops, and archbishops or Popes that can be found in the Christian church. In short, there is no hierarchy to clutter this faith.

ISLAMIC SOCIETY

THE QUR'AN AND ISLAMIC LIFESTYLE

The Islamic religion plays a large part in the everyday life of Muslims, as does the *Qur'an*. The impetus comes from within, where a formidable religious discipline is fostered from birth. The very word Islam means acceptance and surrender, commitment and submission. To every pious Muslim his role is frequently repeated and crystal clear.

The contents of the *Qur'an* provide a guide to life. Where it is contradictory or hazy, the Muslim may turn to the Prophet's *sunnah*—his words or actions as distinct from the revelations—which are recorded in the *hadiths*. Years ago, Islamic scholars sifted through the many and various *hadiths* to eliminate the suspect and preserve a genuine consensus. The collected works are known as the "Six Sound Books." Even today the *Hadith* commands an authority second only to the *Qur'an* and has, for the most part, been accepted without question, even though it was set down some two centuries after the death of Muhammad.

Coupled together, these sources of wisdom provide the rule of law, or *shariah*. The word translates to "pathway" and it is an encompassing code that includes law and moral behavior. It even includes the preferred foods for a Muslim to eat. According to the *shariah* those who commit moral outrages such as adultery, for example, are punished alongside those who steal, although in Western eyes the two "crimes" attract different moral codes.

DIVERGENCE OF TRADITION

Not all Muslim states adhere as vehemently to the *shariah* as they once did and some more familiar rules of law that have been borrowed from the British, French, or Swiss systems have begun to prevail. However, there remains much

Left: Fundamentalist Muslims, typically from Shiah sects, gather at emotionally-charged occasions when breast- or head-beatings are familiar signs of devotion.

Below: Friday prayers remain important for Muslims, even in secular Britain. These worshippers have gathered in Bradford, England, to worship. A little more than one million of the world's estimated 450 million Muslims live in England.

talk of Muslim fundamentalists, those who live strictly by Muslim laws and abhor those who do not. The brooding suspicion with which they view the decadent West, which has both colonially and economically held Muslim countries to ransom, is mutual. Muslim fundamentalists are radical in an already radical religion, but those who make the headlines with hijacks or hostage-takings remain very much a minority. Most Muslims would question the Qur'anic authority for such acts.

However, there is a wide difference between Muslims in terms of social behavior. While all Muslims will abstain from alcohol, the consumption of which might come between man and God, and will not eat pork, there are various interpretations of the dress code. Only the most strict sects will insist on *purdah* for women, that is the covering of the face in public. Muslim parents see it as their duty to choose a suitable partner for their children, but again this is coming under pressure, particularly where Muslims mix freely with other cultures. Polygamy, although practiced by the Prophet, is also coming under scrutiny.

For centuries, two faces of Islam have existed, Sunni and Shiah. The schism occurred soon after the death of Muhammad, when there was controversy over the rightful heir to Islam. The first three *Caliphs*, or guardians of the faith, were Abu Bakr, Umar, and Uthman. This succession was accepted by the Sunnis, who felt the job should go to the most able candidate. However, a different faction believed that the leadership should have remained with Muhammad's family, specifically with Ali ibn Abi Talib, his cousin and son-in-law. This earned them the name of Shiah Ali, the party of Ali. Their dream was finally recognized, but the eventual accession of Ali after the murder

of Uthman brought about its own diplomatic difficulties and soon afterward Ali was killed by the poisoned sword of a Muslim fanatic. His son, Muhammad's grandson, was also killed in a battle near Baghdad, an event still marked by the Shiah. Ali and his descendants are known by the Shi'ites as *imams*.

The Shiah themselves are split on the subsequent number of *imams*. One group, the Ismailis, recognize seven imams, the last being Muhammad ibn Ismail, from whom they take their name. Sometimes they are known as the "seveners." The Assassins, feared warriors of the Middle Ages, were seveners, as are the

present-day Druze Muslims and the followers of the Aga Khan.

In addition there are "twelvers," those who recognize a dozen *imams*, the last of whom, Muhammad Al-Mahdi, remains hidden but will return before Judgment Day.

The Sunnis are in the majority now, as they were at the death of Muhammad, and tend to live in Muslim countries with secular governments. Muslim states where secularism is seen as Satanism are those where Shi'ites predominate.

CHAPTER NINE
SIKHISM

Down the years the message of established religions has frequently been either diluted or polluted. Devout believers may not doubt their faith in God but have grave reservations about the rituals and actions carried out on earth in his name. For this reason new religions have emerged, with varying degrees of staying power.

Even now it takes a great deal of courage to be a convert to a different religion or a new interpretation of God's laws. Years ago when horizons were relatively narrower than they are today it took faith, hope, and bravery in large and equal measures. Sikhism is one example of an alternative path to existing dogmas which has endured. Although still in the minority, even in its homeland of northern India, Sikhism has flourished and spread. Its appeal for many lay in the call for equality between rich and poor and men and women right from its inception. Similarly, its emphasis on providing help for the needy or the search for the soul strikes a chord.

The foundation of Sikhism is attributed to Guru Nanak (1469–1539). To set the scene, however, we should first consider the contribution made in the 15th century by Kabir, a poor weaver who lived in Benares (these days called Varanasi), an Indian city astride the River Ganges.

GURU NANAK

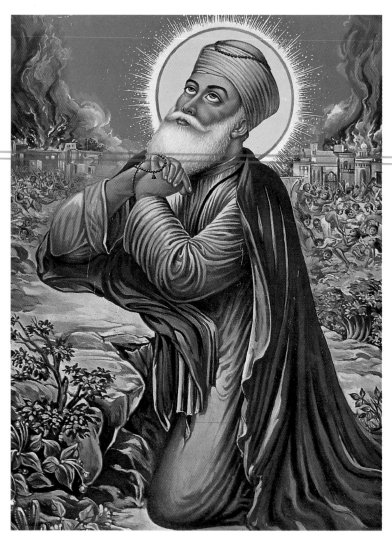

THE BRAVE WEAVER

By faith Kabir was a Muslim but, in stark contrast to many of his brethren, he was inclined toward aspects of Hinduism. Such was his determination to know more that he hid himself in the path of a Hindu teacher who then tripped over him. Kabir subsequently became his disciple.

To the chagrin of the leaders of both religions he then preached that there was truth in both Islam and Hinduism—at a time when the two faiths were bitterly opposed to one another. He was thrown out of Benares for his beliefs but this did not change his message. Instead, at considerable personal risk, he traveled the surrounding countryside broadcasting this revolutionary—almost heretical—view and he gathered followers wherever he went.

It is said that at his death both the Muslims and Hindus wanted his body but all they could find was a wreath of flowers.

Kabir's teachings, expressed in Hindu verses, were soon incorporated into the religious belief known as the Nirguna Sampradaya or the Sant Tradition which was based in northern India. An assortment of religious notions,

it had various recognizable elements including the mysticism of the Sufis, the inner discipline of the Yogis, the poetry of Hinduism, and the monotheism of Islam.

THE PATH OF GOD

Guru Nanak emerged on to the region's religious scene hot on the heels of Kabir. Instinctively he was drawn by Sant ideology but ultimately he picked his own path around the minefield of medieval faith. The result was Sikhism.

Nanak, born a Hindu, had grown up in the village of Talvandi, 40 miles southwest of Lahore, now known as Nankana Sahib. Even as a boy he displayed remarkable wisdom in his treatment of fellow men. His father, an

"There is neither Hindu nor Muslim, so whose path shall I follow? I shall follow God's path. God is neither Hindu nor Muslim and the path which I follow is God's." Guru Nanak.

accountant, once gave him some money and told him to go to a nearby town to trade and profit with it. On the way Nanak encountered a group of holy men who were depressed and hungry. Nanak continued to the town, spent the money on food, and distributed it among the men before he returned home. His father, seeing him empty handed, was furious but Nanak explained that he had put the cash to the best possible use, feeding the hungry.

One day he was praying on the banks of the river when he disappeared. He returned a few days later, apparently struck dumb. When he finally spoke he revealed: "God is neither Hindu nor Muslim and the path which I follow is God's."

He married in Talvandi and fathered two sons before leaving for the town of Sultanpur to work for a local *nawab* or nobleman. In about 1500 he left Sultanpur to wander the country and even beyond in search of the truth about God.

When visiting Mecca he was chastized for lying down with his feet toward the holy Ka'aba. This showed belligerent disrespect to God, he was told. "Turn my feet in a direction where God is not to be found?" he challenged.

He finally settled when he was offered land on the right bank of the River Ravi in the Punjab and it was on this site that he founded the village of Kartarpur where he lived and eventually died. Those who visited him there were known as his *sikhs*, or disciples.

For Nanak the worship of God was very much a matter for the heart. In pursuit of union with God. temple visits, pilgrimages, fasting, and celibacy counted for little, he declared. Only meditation on the wonder of God and his creation was likely to turn a mortal away from meaningless earthly values and toward God.

He taught *nam simran*, rememberance of the divine Name, as a principal route to God, the "Realm of Truth" and freedom for the soul. Many of the teachings he bequeathed are in the form of poetry put to music which are even today chanted in Sikh temples.

Below: **Guru Nanak,** *also pictured left,* **at the moment of his enlightenment. His radical policy of taking religion out of previously prescribed boundaries of either Hindu or Muslim worship perplexed religious leaders but appealed to the people.**

SIKH GURUS

By the time of his death Guru Nanak had gathered a large community of disciples around him at Kartarpur. The question of who would succeed the patriarch began to loom large.

Guru Nanak himself elected the second guru. It was to be Lehna, a long-time follower who distinguished himself by undertaking even the lowliest task with humility and good humor. Nanak changed Lehna's name to Angad, which means "part of me." For the 13 years after Nanak's death Angad was the guru or spiritual teacher for the expanding band of followers whose initial title of Nanankpathis was dropped in favor of Sikhs. Mindful of his predecessor's special significance, Guru Angad collected hymns and wisdom to form a basis for the Sikh scriptures. He was married to Mata Khivi and fathered three children.

It fell to him to choose the third guru. The chosen one, Guru Amar Das, introduced Sikh festivals in an attempt to bind together the community. Borrowing from the Hindu faith he instituted three festival days modifying them sufficiently to become Sikh celebrations as well as distinctive ceremonies for birth, death, and marriage. As it happened he was also the head of a dynasty which thereafter dominated the line of Gurus.

Above: **Guru Hargobind Singh imposed military discipline on his followers to defend the faith.**

His son-in-law, Guru Ram Das, succeeded the title in 1574. During his tenure the town of Amritsar was founded. The youngest son of Ram Das, Arjan, was Guru by 1581 and it was he who began construction of the Golden Temple at Amritsar which was completed in 1601. He established the first home for lepers in India at Tarn Taran. Also he is remembered as the Guru who collected the hymns and prayers of previous gurus into one book.

Sikhism was becoming a victim of its own success. Jealous Muslim Mughal leaders were concerned at its growing success and Guru Arjan was arrested. In 1606 he was tortured and died in captivity, his role being taken by son Guru Hargobind, the sixth Guru and great-grandson of Guru Amar Das. It was he

THE SIKH GURUS	
GURU NANAK	(1469-1539)
GURU ANGAD	(1539-1552)
GURU AMAR DAS	(1552-1574)
GURU RAM DAS	(1574-1581)
GURU ARJAN	(1581-1606)
GURU HARGOBIND	(1606-1644)
GURU HAR RAI	(1644-1661)
GURU HAR KRISHAN	(1661-1664)
GURU TEGH BAHADUR	(1664-1675)
GURU GOBIND SINGH	(1675-1707)

GURU HAR RAI

> "There is but one God, whose name is True, the Creator, devoid of fear and enmity, immortal, unborn, self-existent, great and bountiful; The True One was in the beginning, the True One was in the primal age. The True One is, was, and the True One shall also be." Sikh morning prayer.

who instituted greater political and military organization among the Sikhs than ever before.

The dominance of the family continued when his grandson, Guru Har Rai, came to the post in 1644. He is remembered for opening hospitals which offered free treatment. Guru Har Rai's five-year-old son became guru in 1661 and died just three years later after devoting himself to the care of smallpox victims.

In 1664 Guru Tegh Bahadur was the spiritual leader of the Sikhs at a time when persecution was intensifying. He was martyred in 1675 for insisting everyone should be allowed to worship as they wished at a time when the political will was for conversion to Islam.

Against a troubled background the tenth and final Guru, Gobind Singh, came to prominence in 1675. The changes he made are still manifest in the lives of Sikhs today. In response to the threat of armed incursion into Sikh strongholds, Guru Gobind Singh began a brotherhood which would defend a newly formed Sikh state in the Punjab.

Legend has it that in 1699 at a Sikh assembly he called for five men willing to die for their faith. Soon after each volunteer stepped into a tent the Guru emerged wielding a sword dripping with blood. He revealed he had not in fact slaughtered the loyal disciples but was making them the first members of the militant Khalsa.

Its men were, and still are, distinctive by the 5 ks—*kesh* (uncut hair), *kanga* (the comb for the hair), *kara* (a steel wristband as a reminder that God is one), *kirpan* (a sword with which to defend the helpless), and *kaccha* (short trousers). Observance of the first k involved the use of a turban to keep the long hair in place.

The Khalsa were not just an army, but had moral and religious duties too. They refused alcohol and tobacco. Guru Gobind Singh further changed the surnames of all Sikhs in the Khalsa to match his own which translates to "lion." Women were given the surname Kaur meaning "princess." The aim was to perpetuate the ties that bound Sikhs to their faith and to each other. Nowadays, it is usual for Sikhs to add a family name to avoid confusion.

Baptism into the Khalsa is a complex business and young Sikhs might postpone it until they felt ready to undertake its responsibilities.

There was no successor to the Guru Gobind Singh. Before his death he decreed that the Sikh scriptures in the holy Granth Sahib would be the spiritual guide for future generations.

Right: **Guru Gobind Singh decreed the Granth Sahib would be the guru for future generations.**

With the death of the tenth Guru the era of the living spiritual leader of the Sikhs was ended and the age of the book began. Already the Adi Granth, or first volume, existed thanks to the efforts of the Guru Arjan. It comprised 974 poetic works by Guru Nanak as well as contributions from Ram Das and Arjan himself. When Guru Arjan installed the Adi Granth in the new Sikh temple at Amritsar he bowed before it, illustrating even in those early days that the teaching was more important than the teacher.

Later, scriptures penned by the ill-fated Guru Tegh Bahadur were added and it was finally closed during or soon after the tenure of Guru Gobind Singh. In addition words of wisdom by the Muslim Kabir, the Hindu teacher Jaidev and other important figures from the Sant tradition were included, once again illustrating the open nature of Sikhism.

The sum total of the Guru Granth Sahib or Sikh "Bible" is about 6,000 hymns written by six Gurus, certain Sikh poets of the era, and a dozen non-Sikhs. Most of it is written in *gurmurkhi*, a script said to have been invented by Guru Nanak (the name translates to "pertaining to the Guru"). The Guru Granth

SIKH SCRIPTURES

Above: **The Granth at Amritsar is the oldest and best loved in the world. It is accorded full respect and always remains under cover.**

Sahib starts with the works of the six Gurus in chronological order. Also, they are grouped according to the key in which they are sung.

Guru Nanak himself believed that the true guru was the word of God. Human gurus played a part only in giving expression to that divine word. The authority of the Adi Granth, also known as the Guru Granth Sahib, expanded over the years to become the divine teacher. While Sikhs are not idol worshippers they do venerate the Adi Granth as a kind of catalyst through which they might find purity and piety.

The aim of Sikhs is to abandon *haumai* or egoism to find union with God. *Haumai* comprises lust, anger, vanity, greed, and pride. To do so they concentrate on four key words. First comes the *Nam*, or name, another way by which Sikhs know God, and secondly comes *sabad*, the word. The *guru* or teacher is third with whose help they hope to achieve harmony, *hukam*, the fourth word and final goal. Through the name and the word the worshipper contemplates the true nature of God. With help from the teacher he is enlightened and might then seek harmony in the order of being.

Sikh families are unlikely to have their own copy of the Adi Granth. Instead they might have a *gutka*, a small book containing about 18

of the best-loved hymns. After rising and washing it is usual for the family to assemble and read or hear randomly picked passages. In the home as well as the temple the Granth is treated with reverence, given its own shelf, and usually placed on a cloth or cushion before being used. Above it there will be a canopy, further emphasizing its holiness, and the reader will use a fan or *chauri* to prevent any flies or dust landing on it.

For years Sikhs refused to have the Adi Granth published for fear that, once it became freely available, it would not be treated with due respect. So until the 19th century all the Adi Granths in circulation were written by hand. When Sikhs finally bowed to the pressure of demand and published they decided to make each copy uniform in size and length. All run to 1,430 pages.

The poetry of the Guru Gobind Singh is contained in the Dasam Granth, a revered book but one that is ranked below the Adi Granth. Mostly written in *gurmukhi*, however, it also features work in Sanskrit and Persian, languages mastered by the Guru. This makes it rather difficult to comprehend for most Sikhs. Another poet whose work is used in Sikh worship is Bhai Gurdas, the nephew of the Guru Amar Das.

"My faith is for the people of all castes and all creeds from whichever direction they come and to whichever direction they bow."
Guru Arjan Dev.

SIKH WORSHIP

Few could fail to be moved by the Golden Temple at Armritsar, chief among the religiously significant Sikh sites. Breathtaking in its splendor, the gold leaf which smothers the 16th-century building is reflected mirror-like in the man-made "Pool of Immortality" lying before it.

THE GURDWARA

Every morning the Adi Granth is brought back to the temple at shoulder-height in its protective silver casket from the treasury where it is kept under armed guard at night, for this is the oldest Granth in existence.

It is carried to the causeway before the tranquil lake and placed on a cushion under a canopy in order that a succession of readers can chant verses from it throughout the day. Tradition dictates that worshippers stand before it and bow with hands together before passing on in a clockwise direction.

Sikh temples are known as gurdwaras—"the door of the Guru"—and may be anything from an upstairs bedroom in a regular house to a mighty temple. In essence it is the venue for congregational worship which contains the Adi Granth. Each bears the Sikh flag which features one double-edged sword, two kirpan swords, and a *chakra* or circle representing the oneness of God.

On entering any gurdwara the worshipper goes before the copy of the Granth, the focal point, touches the floor with the forehead and makes an offering of food or money just as he once would have done to a living guru. The gifts are used for the benefit of the community. As he moves away to rejoin the congregation the Sikh never turns his back on the Granth, keen to show the same respect to the book as he would have offered a religious leader.

The key mode of worship is hymn-singing although at certain times the *Ardas*, or Sikh prayer, is recited. (Morning prayer is called *Japji* while evening prayer is *Rehras*.) Not only does the prayer seek divine guidance but it also incorporates the past sufferings and glories of the Sikh community. It ends with the rallying cry of "raj karega khalsa" which translates as "the Khalsa shall rule."

Alcohol and tobacco are forbidden in the vicinity of the temple. Anyone who has consumed alcoholic drink is also not welcome. Before entering it is customary to remove shoes and to insure that the head is covered.

A thanksgiving for a safe birth is given at the temple. Baptism may be carried out either

"Blessed is the place and blessed are those who dwell there, where God's name is meditated upon." Guru Arjan Dev.

in the temple or at home by five Sikhs in the presence of the Adi Granth. Mothers of the newborn are forbidden to prepare food for 40 days to insure they receive adequate rest. Those married in the gurdwara will circle the Granth four times in a clockwise direction as part of the ceremony.

A gurdwara is more than simply a place to pray. It is also a community center offering food and shelter to the poor. There may even be a dispensary. In countries outside India the languages of Urdu or Punjabi are taught there. After a Sikh service the *langar*, a meal, is served free of charge. Demonstrating the equality of the faith, all are invited to the *langar* be they rich, poor, Sikh, or non-Sikh. Similarly, the task of preparing the *langar* falls to men and women.

FESTIVALS
Sikhs follow the Hindu lunar calendar. The only fixed religious festival is Baisakhi, which marks the founding of the Order of Khalsa, which occurs on April 13. It represents a Spring festival and the Sikh New Year.

The martyrdom of the Gurus Arjan Dev and Tegh Bahadur and the birthdays of the Gurus Nanak and Gobind Singh are also celebrated although the dates are movable. The last two festivals involve the reading of the Adi Granth in its entirety, known as Arkhand Path, beginning two days before the date of the festival in order that it may be completed at the appropriate time. These festivals, linked to the gurus, are known as *gurpurbs* while the rest, characterized by fairs and markets, are *melas*.

Below: **The Golden Temple at Amritsar is revered but not worshipped. Sikh scriptures say of God:** "He dwells in everything; he dwells in every heart."

MODERN SIKHISM

An estimated 12 million Sikhs live in India, no more than two percent of the subcontinent's colossal population of 844 million. The vast majority of Sikhs still live in the Punjab or the neighboring state of Haryana. A small percentage are to be found in Delhi while the rest are thinly spread around India.

Left: **An illustration of the violence that characterized "Operation Blue Star," inflicting physical and mental scars on the Sikh community.**

Despite their limited numbers Sikhs have always wielded a disproportionately large influence on Indian affairs mainly because they are drawn from the mercantile classes and also because they dominate in the fertile farming areas. Sikhs have traditionally placed a great deal of emphasis on education, too, which has resulted in Sikhs finding jobs in the upper echelons of the armed forces, in transport, and in political activity.

The Sikhs have known a difficult history. There were numerous skirmishes with the Muslims which were then superseded by battles with the colonial British.

The Punjab lost its independence in 1849 after it was annexed by the British following an unsuccessful Sikh revolt. Afterward, Sikhism became virtually submerged in Hinduism. When it recovered a measure of independence the fraternal relations once known by Sikhs and Hindus were ultimately obliterated, in simple terms, by the frustrated dream of some

Above: **The funeral of Premier Indira Gandhi (1917–1984). Hindus were outraged by her assassination by Sikh extremists.**

Peter Ustinov. On her way she passed two Sikh bodyguards, men she knew and trusted. But Beant Singh and Satwant Singh knew a greater loyalty to their faith than to her. In reply to her smile of greeting Beant Singh fired off three bullets from his revolver. Satwant Singh then turned on her with his sten gun. The 66-year-old premier was rushed to hospital with 10 bullet wounds but could not be saved.

Police who surrounded Beant shot him after he cried: "I have done what I wanted to do. Now do as you please." Satwant, injured but alive, stood trial for Gandhi's murder, was found guilty and hanged. The backlash against the Sikh population from furious Hindus was intense and violent.

The religion has been exported via immigration to the United Kingdom, Canada, Africa, and Malaya. As it spreads among other cultures there comes the desire among some younger members to forsake many of the symbols of their faith, for example the turban which is such a distinctive emblem and recognized throughout the world. Sikhs who have been baptized into the Khalsa and later renege on the 5 ks are called *patit* or "fallen" by their erstwhile brothers. Others who have never been baptized but attempt to follow the teachings of the Sikh gurus are known as *sahaj-dhari* Sikhs, or slow-learners.

radicals to enjoy independence once more. It remains a suggestion strongly resisted by the Indian government.

The issue came to a head in 1984 when Sikh extremists occupied the Golden Temple at Amritsar demanding independence. Prime Minister Indira Gandhi was determined that the borders of Mother India should remain the same and she was equally keen that her authority should be stamped all over the crisis.

In June 1984, she sent her troops in to confront the rebels. Operation Blue Star succeeded in clearing the temple of its protesters but left 700 Sikhs dead, including the leader of the faction, Sant Jarnail Singh Bhindranwale. In addition, 90 soldiers were killed. The aggressive tactics in the holy place were calculated to inflame Sikhs everywhere. Indira Gandhi paid for her actions with her life.

Five months after the rout at the temple, on October 31, 1984, she walked serenely from her office anticipating an interview with actor

SIKHS WEAR DIFFERENT COLORED TURBANS. BLUE SIGNIFIES A MIND AS BROAD AS THE SKY AND IS APPROPRIATE FOR SOMEONE WHO UPHOLDS THE SIKH PRINCIPLES OF EQUALITY. THOSE IN A WHITE TURBAN ARE GOODLY PEOPLE LIVING PRAISEWORTHY LIVES. THE BLACK TURBAN IS A REMINDER OF THE PAST PERSECUTIONS SUFFERED BY THE SIKHS. OTHER COLORS ARE A MATTER OF PERSONAL CHOICE.

CHAPTER TEN
MODERN MOVEMENTS

The world's religious scene is constantly shifting and, as old faiths fall, new ones rush forward to take their place. To some, the very age of a well-established religion gives additional stature; but there is no denying that the fresh approach of a fledgling belief can be irresistible.

A number of successful religions have been launched in the past 150 years. Without exception every one of them has attracted criticism but this is nothing new. Two thousand years ago Christians were demonized by the authorities—and today their faith is the largest in the world! Those who condemn the recent religions often have a vested interest in seeing them fail as the critics are frequently zealous members of a rival faith.

MORMONS

When Joseph Smith (1805–1844) prayed to God for guidance on which church to choose, he was told in a revelation that all were "abominations." Before him stood God the Father and God the Son, who advised Smith that he would emerge as the leader of the one true church.

Above: **Temple Square in Salt Lake City, the spiritual home of Mormonism.**

A second vision some years afterward was, if anything, even more sensational. In 1823, an angel, Moroni, appeared before Smith and commanded him to seek out ancient golden tablets inscribed in an Egyptian dialect and hidden on a hillside near New York. Four years later Smith duly recovered the tablets and set to work transcribing them, with guidance from God and the assistance of a mysterious instrument called the Urim and Thummin, later described as sacred spectacles. Working from behind a screen, Smith dictated the translation and the result was The Book of Mormon, published in 1830.

"As man is, God once was. As God is, man may become."
The Book of Mormon

CHURCH OF THE LATTER DAY SAINTS

The author of the original tablets, which are said to give the religious and secular history of the Western hemisphere from about 2200 B.C. to A.D. 421, was apparently descended from Hebrews who made their way to the United States shortly before the Jews were taken to Babylon.

Although a colony was successfully started by escapees (two of whom came from Jerusalem and one from Babel), the society grew away from God. There ensued a mighty battle between believers and non-believers—and only non-believers survived. These became the native Americans. Smith put the new Mormon faith, soon to be described as the Church of the Latter Day Saints, firmly within the Christian camp.

"The fundamental principles of our religion are the testimony of the Apostles and Prophets concerning Jesus Christ, that He died, was buried, and rose again the third day and ascended into heaven; and all other things which pertain to our religion are only appendages to it." Joseph Smith.

During his tenure at the head of the Mormon Church, Smith had divine authority which was bequeathed to his successors. But critics of Mormonism are quick to point out his personal character defects. Smith was tried in 1826 on the charge of "money-digging," or reckless treasure hunting, which was linked to his lifelong dependence on a seer stone which he felt offered prophetic wisdom.

CRIMES AND MISDEMEANORS

By 1828 Smith had apparently applied for membership of a local Methodist church even though God, Jesus, and an angel had already appeared to him begging him to refrain from joining an existing church.

The historical notions that Smith related in The Book of Mormon appeared in 1825 in a work of fiction called *View of the Hebrews* written by Ethan Smith and published a few miles from where Smith lived.

He died in a shoot-out following a scandal in which he ordered the destruction of a newspaper that had threatened to expose his sexual misdemeanors.

There are other inexplicable twists in the tale woven by Smith, not least that the native Americans are of Asian origin rather than from the Middle East. A number of men who professed to have witnessed the discovery of the golden tablets later renounced Mormonism, insisting they had seen this wonder through the "eye of faith." Other charges against

Mormonism are that it is authoritarian, that it breeds by secret rituals, and that the original truth of the revelation has been doctored countless times to attract converts.

Yet the lifestyle of Mormons is beyond reproach. They avoid tobacco and alcohol and even tea and coffee. Families are closely-knit, with special emphasis placed upon the value of the youth. Householders give ten percent of their earnings to the church as a tithe.

Mormons set great store by their missionary work and, because of it, current membership stands at an estimated 9.5 million, more than half of whom come from outside the United States. Their faith, which decrees that only Mormons will reach the highest heaven, has prompted them to keep accurate genealogical records so that converts can "baptize" their ancestors. The records have helped many a researcher over the years.

SMITH'S SUCCESSOR, BRIGHAM YOUNG, WHO LED MORMONS TO THE PROMISED LAND OF UTAH AND SALT LAKE CITY HAD 17 WIVES AND 57 CHILDREN. HE DEFENDED THE POLYGAMY PRACTICED BY HIS FAITH BY SAYING HE WAS A PROTECTOR RATHER THAN A LOVER.

SPEAKING ABOUT HIS WIVES, YOUNG ADMITTED, "I HAVE 15; I KNOW OF NO-ONE WHO HAS MORE; BUT SOME OF THOSE SEALED TO ME ARE OLD LADIES, WHOM I REGARD RATHER AS MOTHERS THAN WIVES BUT WHOM I HAVE TAKEN HOME TO CHERISH AND SUPPORT."

YOUNG WAS SPIRITUAL LEADER OF THE MORMON CHURCH AND GOVERNOR OF THE STATE OF UTAH WHEN IT JOINED THE UNITED STATES. POLYGAMY WAS OUTLAWED BY THE MORMONS IN 1890.

Most people have heard about Jehovah's Witnesses, perhaps the most zealous missionaries of all. They are familiar figures on doorsteps across the world, politely asking occupants if they would like to talk about God. It is the duty of a Witness to recruit members for the church in a sincere effort to save them from destruction.

JEHOVAH'S WITNESSES

BUYING BACK LIFE

First President of the movement was Charles Taze Russell (1852–1916) whose father owned and ran a haberdashery shop in Allegheny, part of Pittsburgh, Pennsylvania.

Russell's early interest in the Bible was focused on a study group with which he became increasingly involved. By the age of 25 he had given up financial interests in his father's business and become a preacher.

Not all his beliefs fell within the boundaries of the major faiths. He rejected the existence of hellfire but was adamant that Jesus gave his life for sinners. He wrote, "To redeem is to buy back. What did Christ buy back for all men? Life. We lost it by the disobedience of the first Adam. The second Adam (Christ) bought it back with his own life."

In July 1879, Russell began publishing Zion's Watch Tower and Herald of Christ's Presence. Three years later he formed a Bible society, first called Zion's Watch Tower Tract Society and now known as the Watch Tower Bible and Tract Society of Pennsylvania. Its members were Bible students. They needed no money to join.

Russell was convinced that the age would end in 1914, which turned out to be the start of World War I but was without a decisive apocalyptic event. Still the society continued to function at its low level.

On the death of Russell, his successor, Joseph Franklin Rutherford of Missouri, set about extending the religion overseas. The Kingdom of God had been founded in the heavens during 1914, he claimed, and kept the faith of the majority in doing so.

THE RECRUITMENT DRIVE

In 1931 the Society officially took the name "Jehovah's Witnesses," which is taken from a reference in the "Book of Isaiah." Witnesses are great students of the Bible, including the Old Testament and this inspires them to know God as Jehovah. By 1935, they were emphasizing their controversial doctrine that 144,000 Christians would make their way to heaven. The rest would be obedient subjects of the Lord in paradise on earth. The recruitment drive is to people this "great crowd" below the celestial kingdom.

Efforts by Witnesses to spread the word during World War II were severely hampered by Hitler's vehement opposition, fired by the refusal of group members to support the National Socialist Movement or to bear arms. Many were thrown by the Nazis into concentration camps. But the missionary work continued apace after the war with Nathan H. Knorr at the helm. He oversaw the biggest expansion ever in membership.

Membership continued to grow despite the alleged passing of the predicted date for Armageddon in October 1975 and the death of Knorr in 1977.

The faith has a reputation for being joyless as Witnesses do not celebrate birthdays or Christmas, believing both to have roots in pagan festivals. Another point of friction is the prohibition of blood transfusions, even to those who are critically ill. Witnesses believe that importing blood into the body is against God's law.

Witnesses meet for worship at Kingdom Halls. Services are taken by elders as there are no paid clergy and when adults are converted they are baptized into the faith.

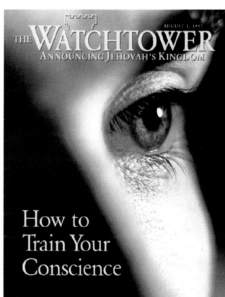

Above: **The** *Watchtower* **magazine is the calling card of missionary Jehovah's Witnesses.**

Left: **Mass baptism, like this one taking place in West London, is the route by which newly made converts enter the Jehovah's Witnesses.**

"When it rains, what do we see? Lightning and thunder! That is the natural world. That is a marriage-like phenomenon in the world of weather. This is Nature's way of marriage. Even though a man by himself as the subject has the assets of Life, Love, Lineage, and Conscience within, nothing happens without his love partner, woman. In order for human beings to have all of this exciting and stimulating plea-sure, the entire creation, beginning with mineral, plant, and animal kingdoms, are being mobilized for that purpose, stage by stage, ulti-mately in order to reach that ideal of God's love." Rev. Sun Myung Moon.

UNIFICATION CHURCH

MR. MOON

In some modern churches the major themes are earthly rather than heavenly. For the Rev. Sun Myung Moon the eradication of Communism comes high on his agenda.

Mr. Moon (in his case the term Reverend is a courtesy title) was born in 1920 in North Korea and grew up in the Presbyterian Church. At the age of 15 he apparently saw Jesus in a vision at Eastertime and was told to continue the good work begun by the Savior almost 2,000 years before. Over the next nine years, he received the wisdom of God, Jesus, Moses, and Buddha, ultimately setting down a new theology in a book he called *The Divine Principle*, ghostwritten by his disciple Yee Hye Wen and published in 1957.

In tandem with his spiritual education, Moon studied to become an engineer, working sometimes in Japan. In 1945 he began preaching, but soon afterward was dispatched to a labor camp by the Communist North Korean government.

His supporters claim he upset the authorities by his daring anti-communist stance. Enemies believe that bigamy and adultery were the real reasons for his incarceration. In any event, it was three years before U.N. forces released him. Moon was at this time nominally representing a fringe Pentecostal group. He was excommunicated from the Presbyterian Church of Korea in 1948.

THE UNIFICATION CHURCH

After Moon moved to South Korea in 1954 he founded the Holy Spirit Association for the Unification of World Christianity. Nowadays outsiders know its members as "Moonies." It is considered a derogatory term and inside the church the title Unificationist is preferred.

Vehemently anti-communist, Moon links Cain, the evil son of Adam and Eve, to left-wing politics, while democracy is spoken of in the same breath as the righteous Abel. Moon's feeling is that God in heaven has capitalist tendencies. In 1972 Moon embarked on a major recruitment drive and moved to the United States—where he was later successfully prosecuted for tax evasion.

The Unification Church is deeply committed to missionary work. Its practice of accosting shoppers in high streets to interest them in the work of the church is by now well-known. The official name of the church does not always identify itself in people's minds as the one run by Moon and missionaries have been known to commit "heavenly deception," to fund themselves. There have been stories of converts being entrapped and brainwashed, with kidnapping and deprogramming carried out by the victims' concerned families.

MASS MARRIAGE

Another feature that has left observers feeling uneasy is the mass weddings, in which hundreds of couples are married, with Moon himself officiating. The marriages are arranged, with church leaders choosing suitable partners. Nuptials are not consummated for three years in order that the blood of offspring is pure.

The Unification Church, with Moon at its head, is indisputably wealthy and owns a large number of religious, political, cultural, and business organizations, including *The Washington Times*.

Unificationists regard God as a single being with "perfect intellect, emotion, and will." The aim is to unite all Christians under one banner. Moon claims the third Adam, a divine and perfect individual, was born in Korea between 1917 and 1930 and that this being is the Second Coming. However, Moon has never claimed to be that person.

"Let us become the soldiers of Heaven who can raise the flag before anyone else and march against Satan." Rev. Sun Myung Moon.

Left: The world's largest mass wedding in which 35,000 couples were married by Sun Myung Moon in the Olympic Stadium in Seoul, South Korea, in August 1995. An additional 325,000 couples took part via a satellite link.

Hand-clapping, drum-slapping, tambourine-smacking monks with shaven heads and saffron robes were once a common sight winding down London's Oxford Street in a column.

KRISHNA
CONSCIOUSNESS

Nowadays the dress code is strictly casual for Krishna monks spreading the word on street corners. Some even don a wig! They give away copies of *Back to the Godhead* in return for a donation. One of the most prominent symbols of their faith is a necklace with 108 beads, each one representing the Hare Krishna mantra.

SWAMI PRABHUPADA (1896–1977)

The roots of the modern Krishna movement lie in the 16th century when the sage Sri Caitanya of Mayapur (1486–1534) was seen as a reincarnation of the Indian god Krishna.

It is his wisdom which survived until the 20th century and was espoused by His Divine Grave A.C. Bhaktivedanta Swami Prabhupada, who is credited with founding Krishna Consciousness.

Prabhupada was born in Calcutta where, in 1922, he met his spiritual master Srila Bhaktisiddhanta Sarasvati Thakur. This much respected master urged the young Prabhupada to spread the word about Krishna in the English language. At the time, of course, little was known about the god outside India.

Following the practical Hindu code of life, Prabhupada began a pharmaceutical company to finance his family. Not until 1950 did he begin to dedicate his life to preaching and nine years later he renounced all material belongings to pursue greater spirituality.

SOCIETY FOR KRISHNA CONSCIOUSNESS

Remembering the words of his master he found a patron who booked him a berth on the steamship Jaladduta, bound for the United States. It was a 35-day passage during which time Prabhupada suffered extreme ill-health, including two heart attacks. Undeterred, he disembarked in New York City, first finding refuge in a Yoga center and later using a donation to rent some headquarters.

"Hare krishna
Hare krishna
Krishna krishna
Hare hare
Hare rama
Hare rama
Rama rama
Hare hare"

Krishna Chant

Above: **Ex-Beatle George Harrison, pictured here in 1970 at a Festival of Indian Arts in London, supported the Krishnas.**

Far left: **A model of Swami Prabhupada is carried into position for worship.**

In Tompkins Square Park he led the first open-air *sankirtan*, or chanting session, ever held outside India and began attracting swarms of disenchanted Westerners. By July 1966 the International Society for Krishna Consciousness (Iskcon) was formed, its members selling *Back to the Godhead*, a publication begun more than 20 years earlier by Prabhupada who wrote and financed it.

By the time of his death in 1977 Prabhupada had created 108 centers worldwide, written 51 volumes of transcendental literature, traveled the world eight times, and initiated 5,000 disciples. Remarkably he slept only three hours a day, surviving on just a handful of food. Perhaps not surprisingly, he is now worshipped daily by Krishnas.

CULTURAL ENDEAVORS

Living in temples and farm communities, Krishnas vow to refrain from gambling, illicit sex, intoxicants, including tea, coffee, and cigarettes, and non-vegetarian food. Adherence to the restrictions of Krishna Consciousness has enabled a number of drug addicts to kick the habit, earning the movement praise from some of the U.S.'s civic dignitaries.

Chanting of the holy name is the fundamental route to Krishna. The chant has a familiar ring thanks to ex-Beatle George Harrison's, 1971 number one hit "My Sweet Lord" which was a tribute to krishna.

Krishna Consciousness sees itself as a cultural movement which, although committed to missionary work, does not seek to defeat other religions. Although they share a god, it is not associated with Hinduism.

Critics point to the harsh regime imposed on converts who rise at between 3 a.m. and 4 a.m. and spend the day either at prayer, doing chores, or selling on the streets. The movement has endured its fair share of scandals. In 1987, leading light James Immel was found beheaded in the back of a shop in London, England. The killer, another disciple, had been disillusioned at tales of Immel's drug-crazed sex sessions.

Prabhupada earned some enmity when he described women as "prone to degradation, of little intelligence, and untrustworthy."

SCIENTOLOGY

When is a philosophy no longer a philosophy? When it becomes a religion. That is what happened to Scientology, the system of beliefs founded by writer L. Ron Hubbard in the middle of the 20th century. His aim was for everyone to achieve happiness by improving self-awareness; there was no divine revelation or vision at the heart of his message, but Hubbard's followers deemed his work so miraculous and spiritually satisfying that it was worthy of church status.

In 1954, Scientologists in Los Angeles established the first Church of Scientology and others sprang up in the United States, the United Kingdom, and eventually across six continents. Although Hubbard is long dead, Scientology church services are haunted by his presence as selections from the 3,000 tape-recorded lectures he left are regularly played.

Lafayette Ron Hubbard (1911–1986) was born in Nebraska, the son of a naval commander and a teacher. At the age of two, he moved with his family to Montana where he mastered horsemanship. He also fostered a close rela-

> "A civilization without insanity, without criminals and without war, where the able can prosper and honest beings can have rights and where man is free to rise to greater heights." The stated aim of L. Ron Hubbard.

tionship with resident Blackfoot peoples and learned many of their ancient ways. From his teacher mother he inherited a love of learning, and from his father his yearning to travel.

As a young man, before he completed his formal education, Hubbard traveled extensively in the Far East and the Pacific, fascinated yet perplexed by the different cultures he encountered. While their rites and rituals were intriguing, he felt none tackled the misery of the human condition.

THE X FACTOR

He was 19 before he returned to study mathematics, engineering, and, later, nuclear physics at George Washington University. He quickly became disillusioned with the academic indifference to matters of the mind. Once again he embarked on a globe-trotting trip to answer

Above: **The Church of Scientology in Clearwater, Florida.**
Left: **Multi-talented L. Ron Hubbard finds relaxation in making music.**

the questions that plagued him. "I suddenly realized that survival was the pin on which you could hang the rest of this with adequate and ample proof. It's a very simple problem. Idiotically simple! That's why it never got solved," Hubbard decided.

"Life, all life, is trying to survive. And life is composed of two things; the material universe and an X factor. And this X factor is something that can evidently organize and mobilize the material universe."

During World War II, Hubbard served in the U.S. Navy in the Pacific and the Atlantic, sustaining eye and spine injuries. He claims to have used the power of his mind to effect his cure and observed other veterans doing the same. After his recovery from his war wounds he wrote *The Original Thesis*, now known as *The Dynamics of Life*, and passed it around among friends. His ideas on developing the mind became known as Dianetics.

THE OFFICE OF SPECIAL AFFAIRS
In 1950 he published *Dianetics: The Modern Science of Mental Health*. Until then he was probably best known as a writer of science fiction, but his book on Dianetics became a bestseller and, before the year was out, 750 groups across the U.S. had been formed to apply his theories.

In 1959, Hubbard and his family moved to Saint Hill Manor in East Grinstead, England,

Above: **Always ready to explore an alternative view Hubbard here measures the electricity in tomatoes. His pet theory of Dianetics allegedly promoted the welfare and wellbeing of millions.**

which became the worldwide headquarters of the Church of Scientology. Seven years later he resigned his position as executive director of the church and, until 1975, he sailed the seas, pioneering a drugs rehabilitation program.

Scientology has been subjected to extensive criticism and has been accused of using mind-bending techniques to keep members from leaving. In reply, Scientologists established an intelligence agency called the Office of Special Affairs which allegedly uncovered scandals to embarrass the British and U.S. governments.

RASTAFARIANS

Black people outside Africa have been pursued by a troubled history and only recently have they channeled their suffering and resentment into a religion which they could call their own.

Rastafarians are distinguishable by their dreadlocks—hair that is neither combed nor cut—and garments of red, black, green, and gold which symbolize Ethiopia, the promised land of the Rastafarians. There are Rastafarians in England and the United States, but the majority live in Jamaica.

The movement is closely linked to black nationalism, an idea propagated back in the 1920s by Jamaican Marcus Mosiah Garvey (1887–1940). He launched the Universal Negro Improvement Association in a bid to encourage fellow Jamaicans back to their African homeland from which they were taken against their will as slaves centuries before. Jamaicans were poor and oppressed. The notion of a homeland where they would find peace and dignity was naturally appealing. Garvey went so far as to predict that a black king would be crowned in Africa who would welcome the blacks home.

THE LION OF JUDAH

Little came of Garvey's Association, although he succeeded in establishing the African Orthodox Church in New York. He died in obscurity in England—but not before the apparent fulfillment of his dreams.

Ten years before Garvey's death, Emperor Haile Selassie was crowned in Ethiopia and was lauded with titles such as Lord of Lords, King of Kings, Ras Tafari, and Lion of Judah. This was enough to persuade nationalist blacks that their living god had taken the throne. Selassie was the Rastafarian god or "Jah," a word probably taken from Jehovah or Jahweh. Rastafarianism came to represent a protest against poverty and persecution.

As for Selassie, he was a Christian rather than a Rastafarian. Born Tafari Makonnen on July 23, 1892 in eastern Ethiopia, he was the son of a royal adviser who at a young age showed an extraordinary talent for languages and Bible study. Aged 14, he was appointed the Governor of the province of Solali, eventually became Regent and King before finally being crowned Emperor. He was forced to flee Ethiopia when Mussolini's armies invaded, but

was reinstated by the Allies in 1941, ruling until his death in 1974. Although he was an autocrat, Ethiopia was extensively modernized under Haile Selassie's rule.

ZION YOUTH

Rastafarians have little doctrine or ritual. They interpret passages of the Bible to illustrate the case for Rastafarianism—perhaps their biggest argument with established Christianity is the portrayal of Jesus as a blue-eyed European. With some justification, they claim this cannot be the case, although insisting that he was a black man is possibly equally fanciful.

Bizarre though it seems, the closest the Rastafarians have to a sacrament is smoking cannabis, a drug banned in most Western countries. By observing this aspect of their religion, many Rastafarians find themselves in trouble with the law and they call the authorities who would punish them for this religiously-inspired misdemeanor "Babylon."

One of the best known Rastafarians was the singer Bob Marley, who sang about an "Exodus" of his people to Africa. The Zion he spoke of was in fact Ethiopia. Although the hope of many is to return to Africa, it seems it is more of a term for spiritual satisfaction than the actual place itself.

BAHA'I

Fast-growing and thriving, the moderate Baha'i faith is one of the recent success stories of the religious world. It's a story in two stages: in May 1844 a young Persian Siyyid Ali Muhammad (1801–1850) revealed that he was the promised messenger, or Qa'im, of Shi'ah Islam. Assuming the title of The Bab (Gate), he was, he declared, an independent messenger preparing the way for the coming of a prophet. That day, May 23, remains a festival for the Baha'is.

THE COMING OF THE BABIS

The Bab attracted not only numerous followers, but also the hostility of the Persian regime. He was imprisoned and shot in July 1850 on the orders of the government in an act of mass oppression which claimed the lives of a further 15,000 recent converts. The first crucial stage in the story of the Baha'is was over.

One of the converts—Babis as they were known—was Mirza Husayn-'Ali, born in 1817. In 1863, after a revelation from God, he announced himself as "the Promised One." He adopted the name Baha'u'llah, meaning "the glory and splendor of God" and followers afterward became known as Baha'is.

There was, however, some dissent, not least from Baha'u'llah's own brother. The quarrelsome pair were exiled first from Tehran, then Baghdad, afterward from Constantinople and Adrianople, until Baha'u'llah was finally imprisoned in Acre, Palestine. Although he was eventually released from jail, he spent the rest of his life in Acre, near Haifa, which is where the Baha'i religion today has its headquarters.

At the death of Baha'u'llah in 1892, his eldest son Abdu'l-Baha assumed control of

"All these divisions we see on all sides, all these disputes and opposition, are caused because men cling to ritual and outward observances, and forget the simple, underlying truth. It is the outward practices of religion that are so different, and it is they that cause disputes and enmity— while the reality is always the same, and one. The Reality is the Truth, and truth has no division. Truth is God's guidance, it is the light of the world, it is love, it is mercy. These attributes of truth are also human virtues inspired by the Holy Spirit." Abdu'l-Baha.

the new and increasingly popular religion. Although he was not considered an earthly manifestation of God, as his father had been, it was believed that his thoughts were divinely inspired. His writings, along with those of the Bab and Baha'u'llah, make up the scriptures of the Baha'i faith.

Abdu'l-Baha's grandson, Shoghi Effendi, took over as the leader of the faith and it was under his leadership that the religion became known throughout the world.

Today the Baha'is are unswervingly democratic. Globally, each area has nine-member boards, known as Local Spiritual Assemblies, elected annually to look after religious affairs. The next tier comprises National Spiritual Assemblies, once again voted in every year by the Baha'is of that country. The pinnacle of the hierarchy is the Universal House of Justice, located in Haifa, Israel, its nine members elected every five years by members of the National Spiritual Assemblies.

PRO LOGIC

Baha'i beliefs are seductively reasonable. If religion is the cause of war, then it is better to have no religion at all, the Baha'is believe. Every age has its own prophets sent by God to help the religion of the world evolve. Differences of opinion are encouraged and

should be resolved by discussion, but it is not permissible to belittle the beliefs of another. There is equality between men and women, rich and poor, and prejudice is an alien concept to the Baha'is.

Such is their conviction in the worth of independent investigation of the truth that there are no clergy to instill doctrine. The Baha'is have even bridged the gap between religion and science, that gray area that has caused so many faiths to stumble.

"Religion and science are the two wings upon which man's intelligence can soar into the heights, with which the human soul can progress. It is not possible to fly with one wing alone." Abdu'l-Baha.

Left: **The striking Baha'i temple in Haifa, northwest Israel, the home of the Baha'i faith.**

Above: **Acre, a Mediterranean port, was allocated as an Arab territory when Israel was created but fell to the Jews in 1948. Years before it was the base of Baha'u'llah, the follower of the Bab, who gave his name to the faith.**

EAST MEETS WEST

Some religions seek to unite the beliefs of East and West, to find God through mysticial insight or self-examination. During the past hundred years, two such creeds have won worldwide recognition, both with their roots in divinity—"The Work," pioneered by Georgei Ivanovitch Gurdjieff (1866–1949), and theosophy are mind-expanding philosophies that demand concentrated study and take years to master.

Right: **Helena Petrovna Blavatsky, known as H.P.B., a champion of esoteric Eastern knowledge.**

Far right: **The enigmatic Gurdjieff required students to perform a stylized dance as they sought higher conciousness.**

Theosophy is derived from two Greek words, *theos* meaning god or divinity, and *sophia* meaning wisdom. The doctrine of theosophy underwrites the basic ideals of organized religion, science, and philosophy and is a confluence of Hindu, Muslim, Buddhist, and Christian thought.

THE THEOSOPHICAL SOCIETY

Its champion was clairvoyant Helena Petrovna Blavatsky (1831–1891), born in the Ukraine to an army colonel and a novelist. From 1849, she embarked on more than 20 years of globe-trotting, during which she encountered numerous mystic traditions.

Unable to find a niche for her findings H.P.B., as she was known, launched the Theosophical Society in July 1875, in conjunction with the journalist and lawyer Henry Steel Olcott (1832–1907) and the American attorney William Q. Judge. At about the same time she

"Take the understanding of the East and the knowledge of the West— and then seek." G.I. Gurdjieff.

wrote her first major work *Isis Unveiled*, which was published in 1877.

Together with Olcott, Blavatsky left the United States for India in 1878 to study theosophical practices in the East. She was concerned to find many of the ancient aspects of religion were being abandoned in favor of Western ways. Blavatsky had a great respect for the esoteric wisdom of Eastern religions and worked hard to preserve it. She was also fascinated by Western mysticism, including Gnosticism, the Kabbalah, and Rosicrucianism, although at the same time she sought to expose idle superstition.

In 1884, Blavatsky was subjected to a smear campaign by ex-employees who accused her of fraud relating to the supernatural powers she claimed to possess. This included her apparent communication with ancient masters who allegedly transmitted wisdom to her from their Himalayan hideouts. The Society for Psychical Research conducted an investigation and found her guilty of the charges. In 1986, however, the S.P.R. belatedly decided that the tests carrried out in its name were flawed.

THE SECRET DOCTRINE

This was not the only source of criticism. Theosophy had existed through the ages in different forms. There were a number of influential theosophists at the time who opposed the Theosophical Society, claiming it was merely a random collection of followers of Eastern thought combined with spiritualism.

The strain of the accusations together with the adverse climate of India finally forced H.P.B. back to London, England, where she lived until her death. The work that best reveals her thoughts and views is *The Secret Doctrine*, although a later book, *The Key to Theosophy*, outlined the components of the movement she cherished, including reincarnation and karma. Since the death of Blavatsky in 1891, the Theosophical Society has undergone many different incarnations, but has survived to publish many works on the concepts of present-day theosophy.

GENIUS, FANTASIST, OR FAKE?

Gurdjieff, born of Greek and Armenian parentage on the Russian-Turkish border, has always aroused strong passions. He knew of Blavatsky's work, but pursued his own highly individual course rather than embrace another's ideas. His words and work were enigmatic. The riddles he posed were translated by Pyotr Demianovitch Ouspensky (1878–1947) into teaching form during a short-lived partnership with Gurdjieff.

It's difficult to summarize Gurdjieff's broad message—there are three principles which appertain to "The Work:" "Know yourself," "Nothing is too much," and "Verify everything for yourself." Pursuit of "The Work" requires immense self-discipline. According to Gurdjieff most people live their lives in a kind of waking

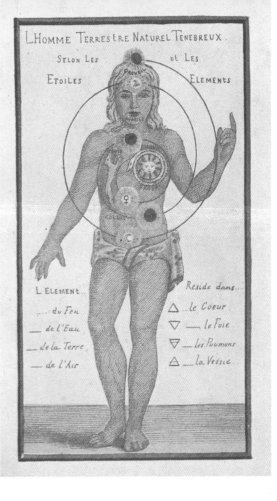

Above: A 19th-century illustration indicating the body's *chakras*, points at which energies from the universal life force enter, are transformed and distributed. They are only visible with clairvoyance.

sleep. Through his "Work" they will find heightened levels of vitality and awareness.

"The Work" is an oral tradition, the understanding of which can only be transmitted by a teacher to a pupil. However, in short, Gurdjieff calls for the resistance of negative emotions. For example, after criticising someone, he advises that you ponder what was said and then apply it to yourself. This neturalizes the poisonous elements of the personality.

So "The Work" seeks higher conciousness and self-realization, together with the eradication of false personality, all of which demand patience and integrity. Gurdjieff, a heavy drinker, attracted criticism not for his obscure sentiments, but for his treatment of disciples which was often harsh and humiliating. This was, he contended, entirely necessary to achieve results.

According to one observer, "'The Work' is something that lives in the hearts of men and women—if they can find it."

Seven Principles of Spiritualism
(According to the British-based
Spiritualists' National Union)

The Fatherhood of God
The Brotherhood of Man
The Communion of Spirits and the
    Ministry of Angels
The Continuous Existence of the
    human Soul
Personal Responsibility
Compensation and Retribution
    hereafter for all the good and evil
    deeds done on Earth
Eternal Progress open to every
    human Soul

SPIRITUALIST CHURCH AND THE CHRISTIAN SCIENTISTS

"As the sunflower turns its face to the light of the sun, so Spiritualism turns the face of Humanity to the light of truth." National Spiritualist Association of Churches in America.

To some, the activities of the Spiritualist Church provide conclusive proof of the goodness of God. To others it is nothing better than a disgraceful fraud.

Spiritualism has been with us since the middle of the 19th century. It began with a family plagued by mysterious rapping sounds. The noises which occurred in the home of the Fox family in Hydesville, New York, appeared to be directed at two of the children, Maggie and Kate. After formulating a code, the pair apparently discovered the knocking was made by the spirit of a pedlar murdered in that very

house years before. In communication with the spirit world, the girls were told, "You have been chosen to go before the world to convince the sceptical of the great truth of immortality."

POPULAR SPIRITUALISM

The girls, who grew up to give public performances of mediumship around America and Europe, were closely scrutinized, but no evidence of deception was ever found. In later life Margaret confessed that the rappings sounds were nothing more than a hoax, although, for some unknown reason, she later withdrew her statement. Both sisters died destitute, but not before a new religion had been born.

Vast numbers of mediums allegedly in touch with the spirit world began to practice

and soon churches sprang up to house them. The first churches in England opened their doors in 1865, while in the United States it was even earlier. At this time psychical research and the new religion of Spiritualism were very much intertwined.

Popularity of Spiritualism was at its height during World War I when many bereaved families sought consolation from "the other side." Its supporters included Sir Arthur Conan Doyle, creator of Sherlock Holmes, and Sir Oliver Lodge, the physicist, both of whom lost sons in the fighting. However, widespread support waned, partly due to the deceptions practiced by some mediums which were publicly exposed, but there are thriving Spiritualist Churches in Britain, the United States, Australia, Brazil, and other countries.

Many people continue to take comfort from the notion that the dead live on, and

Spiritualists claim there is overwhelming evidence for this as demonstrated in mediumship. Both the Spiritualists' National Union in Britain and the National Spiritualist Association of Churches (NSAC) in the U.S. recognize the existence of God. The NSAC, which is a member of the Parliament of World Religions, phrases it like this, "We believe in Infinite Intelligence. We believe that the phenomena of Nature, both physical and spiritual are the expression of Infinite Intelligence."

Both agree that, after death, man reaps as he has sown, although there is no hell and there always remains the opportunity for redemption. Perhaps the biggest bonus for followers of the Spiritualist Church is that the fear of death is entirely removed.

Controversy over Spiritualist Churches in England died down after 1951 when the last Witchcraft Act, under which mediums had once been criminally charged, was repealed. However, the subject of psychic healing remains contentious.

CHRISTIAN SCIENTISTS

The supernatural power of faith and prayer in healing forms the basis of the Church of Christian Science, begun by devout Christian Mary Baker Eddy in 1875. Thrice-married Eddy (1821–1910) was convinced that it was Bible study that healed her of a serious injury in 1866, caused by a fall on an icy pavement. Despite troubles in the early years when she was branded a witch, accused of plagiarism, and sued for fraud, the number of Christian Scientists grew to reach 100,000 by the time of her death. The movement has continued to boom, with members avoiding traditional medicines in favor of treatment from Christian Science practitioners. Their places of worship are defined by an accessible reading room which contains relevant literature.

Above: **Spiritualists spread their hands in the hope of getting in touch with entities from another world.**

Right: **Mary Baker Eddy was critically injured when she fell on an icy pavement but thought her faith brought about a cure.**

Left: **A chair was left for Sir Arthur Conan Doyle at the Spiritualist meetings held in the Royal Albert Hall, London, even after his death, so convinced was he that he would return.**

CULTS

The cults lurk on the fringes of mainstream and modern religions. Small, wayward, sometimes downright wacky, such sects tend to attract more in the way of poor publicity than they do recruits. Their primary theme is often a common one, the love of God. But this consuming emotion in people is too often manipulated and exploited by leaders who may themselves be victims of gross self-delusion. New religions are also recognized as being financially lucrative, as gullible believers have a history of handing over large sums. Cults operate outside the traditional Christian denominations.

THE NOTORIOUS C. O. G.

One of the most notorious is the Children of God. Its founder was David Brandt Berg (1919–1994), also known as Father David or Moses David to his followers. Together with his wife and teenage children, Berg began a ministry at Huntingdon Beach, California, in 1968, specially designed to appeal to the youth culture. By the end of 1969, the media had dubbed the mushrooming group "The Children of God." Within four years there were 130 Children of God communities around the world.

In 1978, it changed its structure and its name to The Family of Love and is now known as The Family. According to The Family its members have spread the Gospel to more than 200 million individuals, a staggering statitistic. Berg said he aimed to leave people "mad, sad, or glad"—but never indifferent. A reclusive figure, Berg communicated with his followers in hundreds of letters which contained his thoughts and teachings.

His philosophy of "loving the sinner, not the sin" was interpreted as a free love, wife-switching, and pornography-tolerant regime. Many of the cult members are children, the result of a "hookers for Christ" campaign in which women would have sex with potential converts to boost numbers.

THE SEX CULT

Another cult which made headlines because of its prediliction for free love was that run by Baghwan Rajneesh. The Baghwan (which translates to "master of the vagina") was brought up by middle-class grandparents in India and went on to teach at the University of Jabalpur where he pioneered a form of meditation which revolved around nudity, love-making, and making loud noises. His first *ashram,* which opened in Poona, India, in 1974, became a Mecca for hippies.

He moved to Oregon in 1981 where he lived in luxury. When he died in 1990, it was rumored that he was suffering from AIDS. The movement he spawned was later known as Osho. It has been severely rationalized, leaving only a few centers open. The success of the Baghwan came even though he was out of step with general hippy conciousness. "That the materially poor can ever be spiritual is out-and-out absurd," he once said.

More mainstream, but nonetheless contro-versial, is the Jesus Army. Its founder was Noel Stanton, who experienced "baptism in the holy spirit" at Bugbrooke, Northamptonshire, England, during the 1970s. He launched the Jesus Fellowship which initially came under the umbrella of the Baptists and Evangelical Church, but it was expelled in 1986 for "isola-tionism." The same year the Jesus Army was formed, with missionaries in combat jackets and crew cuts setting to work at rallies and demonstrations with the aim of attracting the interest of young men. An offshoot of the Fellowship is the "House of Goodness" chain of wholefood stores.

CULT FEVER

The array of cults is broad. There is Emin, or The Eminent Way, revealed to encyclopedia salesman Raymond Armin in 1970 under an oak tree on Hampstead Heath, London. In a newspaper interview, Armin, who now lives in Florida, said, "I reckon I'm about the most bril-liant man you have ever met. I must be to have all these people with university degrees follow-ing me . . ."

Another salesman, Herbert W. Armstrong, started the Worldwide Church of God in 1941. It disintegrated in the 1970s amid claims of financial irregularities and false prophecies. Paul Twitchell (1908–1971) launched Eckankar, proclaiming himself to be the 971st Living Eck Master bringing "a timeless and universal

Right: **The Baghwan Rajneesh in touch with disciples. His broadly-based doctrines left the poor in the cold.**

"If what we do is in love, against such things there is no law. All things are lawful unto me and to the pure all things are pure." David Berg.

truth" about God. Moral Rearmament, started by Frank Buchanan (1878–1961), strived for the five Cs—conviction, contrition, confession, conversion, and continuance. Each cult has different nuances regarding the message of God. None has yet swayed the majority.

THOU SHALT NOT LIE

The biggest disappointment for a new convert is a prophecy that does not come true. The Seventh Day Adventists discovered this to their cost when their elders predicted an apocalypse in 1843—and nothing happened. The congre-gations left in droves. An S.D.A. off-shoot, the Branch Davidians, fell into the same trap in 1959 when they promised the Second Coming. It turned out to be another non-event and the church was sued by many former members who had bought land at the site where it was prophesied to occur.

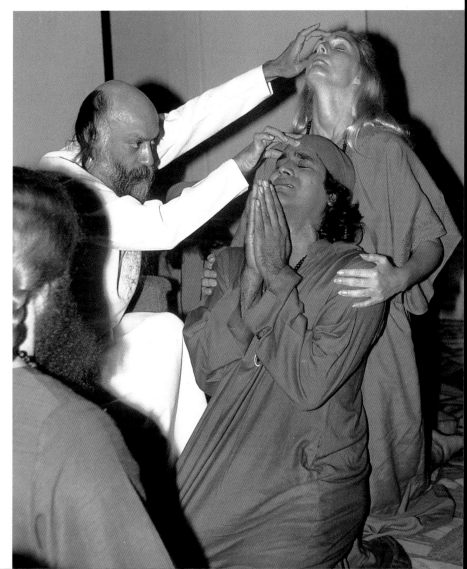

While religion is generally viewed as being benign, there is a flip side inspired by no less an authority than the Bible itself. According to the "Book of Revelation" in the New Testament, Armageddon is the site and title of the final and conclusive battle between good and evil. Some Christians have linked this firmly with the Second Coming, the much-heralded return to earth of Jesus, and the apocalyptic occurrences that will surely accompany this momentous event.

Rev. Jim Jones

DESTRUCTIVE CULTS

The notions are bleak and fraught with suggestions of violence and death. These cults are invariably led by Charismatic leaders with a talent for vivid oratory that can bring such matters to life in the minds of the anxious; hence the "doomsday" cults are born.

DOOMSDAY ... AGAIN

Probably the most notorious of all destructive cults was that led by Jim Jones. The People's Temple Church was founded by Jones, who began to call himself "God's heir on earth." In 1964 he galvanized his followers by predicting the outbreak of a thermonuclear war on July 15, 1967. They followed him in droves from the church's base in Indiana to northern California where Jones assured them they would be safe. Of course, the prophecy remained unfulfilled. Even so, Jones was tempted to try the same trick again a decade later, this time predicting widespread persecution for his followers. They followed him once more, this time to an unforgiving patch of jungle in Guyana purchased by Jones for his perfect society.

Jones had a veneer of respectability and he even dined with Rosalyn Carter when she was the First Lady at the White House. Yet his disciples were verbally and sometimes phsyically abused. As happened in many other cults, their self-esteem was systematically annihilated. The living conditions for devout followers of the cult, particularly in Guyana, were atrocious, yet escape from the watchful eyes of the zealous guards was virtually impossible. Although he began as a devout Christian, Jones began to undermine the authority of the Bible, calling specific verses and parables into question and leaving committed Christians with a gap in their lives which he alone seemed able to fill.

Matters came to a hideous climax when U.S. Congressman Leo Ryan flew to Jonestown in Guyana with journalists and concerned relatives in November 1978. Jones appeared happy to entertain the determined politician, until more than 20 hitherto faithful followers elected to return to America.

There was a scuffle, followed by a dash for the plane, and then bullets began to fly. Ryan was shot dead along with three journalists and three defectors. Immediately Jones summoned the exhausted members of his church around him and urged them to follow him in "a revolutionary act," committing suicide

"If the Bible is true then I am Christ," David Koresh.

through poison. His aides served up Kool Aid laced with cyanide which 912 followers swallowed either by choice or under duress. The dead included 260 children and babies. Jones himself died from a bullet.

FROM WACO TO HEAVEN'S GATE

There are parallels with the Branch Davidians and their hypnotic leader David Koresh, who died in 1993 following a seige at Waco in Texas. Both had delusions of being God's special envoy on earth—Koresh called himself "the sinful Messiah"—and both infected followers with paranoia about the authorities.

The seige at Waco began on February 28, 1993 when four agents from the Bureau of Alcohol, Tobacco, and Firearms died in a shoot-out as they tried to enter the Branch Davidian compound, Mount Carmel, to serve warrants. Koresh's men were well armed. For the next 51 days, the FBI negotiators tried threats, bribes, and pleas, but the negotiations were unsuccessful. The situation was only resolved when flames engulfed Mount Carmel —82 of the faithful died.

Two other destructive cults made headlines during the 1990s. The Order of the Solar Temple was a secretive sect which believed that their leader Joseph di Mambro was the reincarnation of one of the Knights Templar who fought in the Crusades, returned to lead them to salvation on the planet Sirius. While the followers dressed bizarrely in Crusader-style robes, nothing rang warning bells until the simultaneous suicides of 53 followers in Switzerland and Canada on October 5, 1994. Just over a year later more bodies were found in the French Alps, while March 1997 brought five more deaths in Quebec. Some of the bodies were discovered in star formations. Most members were distinguished by being middle-class and affluent. Rumors that followers were murdered and that the leaders of the cult faked their own deaths persist.

Marshall Herff Applewhite, leader of the Heaven's Gate cult, mixed slants of Christianity with large doses of U.F.O.-mania to attract followers, some of whom were recruited on the Internet. On March 26, 1997 a total of 30 of his followers, all dressed in black trousers and new Nike trainers, sporting short hair cuts and bearing five dollar bills in their pockets, took their own lives or were helped to do so. "Planet earth is about to be recycled," declared Applewhite. "The only chance to evacuate is to leave with us."

GLOSSARY

Agape: Communal evening meal shared among the early Christians sometimes translated as "love feast."

Ahisma: Jain term for non-violence.

Alchemy: Forerunner of chemistry, its practitioners sought to turn base metals into gold and to discover the elixir of life.

Angels: Divine messengers to mankind featuring in Christian, Jewish, Islamic, and Zoroastrian faiths.

Apostle: Missionary who preaches the gospel, usually used to describe the dozen disciples of Jesus and St. Paul.

Aryans: Ancient people of central Asia whose descendants spread through Europe and India bringing with them their own language and culture which merged with those of the indigenous tribes.

Asceticism: Stringent self-discipline.

Ashram: A community dedicated to Hindu spiritual teaching.

Atonement: Act which makes the worshipper at one with God,

Avesta: Zoroastrian scriptures.

Cairn: Memorial constructed of boulders piled on top of one another.

Cathars: Heretical sect in southern France which rejected the church as corrupt and finally fell victim to a Papal Crusade.

Ch'i: Chinese universal life principle.

Cult: EITHER a religious sect OR devotion to a particular aspect of a religion, for example, the cult of the Virgin Mary within Christianity.

Dakhma: A "tower of silence" where the Zoroastrians commit their dead whose bodies will be consumed by wild birds or animals. Zoroastrians reject cremation or burial as they see it as a violation of the elements and the earth.

Dharma: In Buddhism, the teaching of the Buddha and route to enlightenment, known as *dhamma* in Pali, the ancient language of Buddhism. In Hinduism it relates to the responsibilities of the castes.

Diaspora: Dispersion of the Jews which began with the exile to Babylon and accelerated with the Roman destruction of Jerusalem in A.D. 70.

Dolmen: Megalithic tomb.

Druid: Priestly order of the Celts best remembered for their involvement in human sacrifice. The Druids of ancient history are unrelated to the Orders of Druids which exist today.

Enlightenment: The realization of great or divine truth.

Feng Shui: Chinese art combining mysticism, science, and superstition to determine good fortune, beneficial sites, and signs and harmony with nature.

Ghat: Broad steps on the banks of the River Ganges, selected ones are used for cremation.

Gnostic: Religious ideas based on spiritual mysticism, regarded as heretical between the first and third centuries by Christians and Jews.

Guru: Indian teacher, translating to "someone who leads you to the light."

Hadith: Muhammad's words and deeds collected in volumes after his death, the most authoritative being the Sahih written by Abu Abdullah Muhammad al-Bukhari in the ninth century.

Holy Spirit: Life force of God.

I Ching: Chinese book of divination and cosmic conciousness.

Icon: Devotional image, either sculpture or painting, of the spirits, saints, or the Holy family venerated by the faithful.

Iconoclast: One who opposes the use of icons in religion, believing it detracts from the worship of God and encourages idolatory.

Jesuit: A member of the Roman Catholic order, the Society of Jesus, founded by St. Ignatious Loyola in 1540. Run with a religious hierarchy its leader is known as the General and is answerable only to the Pope. It was famed for its missionary work.

Karma: Belief that to every action there is a consequence in later life. In Hindu belief this will effect how one is reincarnated.

Mennonites: Protestant Christian denomination founded in 16th-century Holland by Menno Simons.

Messiah: The annointed one, as promised by the prophets of the Old Testament.

Miracle: Event or sequence of events outside the realms of natural law and attributed to God, gods, or supernatural powers.

Missionary: One who seeks to convert those in a different faith to his own.

Moai: Mysterious giant statues on Easter Island in the South Pacific.

Monotheistic: Belief in one all-powerful Creator or God.

Monachism: Monastery system which has monks in isolation or part of the community.

Muezzin: Man who calls Muslims to prayer.

Naman: Painted mark of three vertical lines on the forehead distinguishing a Vaishnavite.

Neanderthal: Primitive man with sloping forehead and large brows; lived in paleolithic or Stone Age Europe.

Nirvana: Perfect enlightenment, unity with bliss, from the Sanskrit word meaning "extinction."

Occult: Hidden or secret knowledge, usually relating to the supernatural and strongly associated with secret rites and ceremonies.

Orthodox: Although it means the holding of acceptable views it is normally used in relation to the Eastern branch of Christianity or a particular Jewish tradition.

Pentateuch: First five books of the Old Testament, also called Torah.

Polytheistic: Belief in numerous gods.

Proselyte: One who converts from one religion to another, originally specific to Judaism.

Religion: A system of faith and worship.

Revelation: EITHER knowledge disclosed to man by divine or supernatural sources OR the last book of the New Testament.

Rishis: Ancient sages who "heard" the Vedas.

Rosary: Circle of beads used as aid to prayer in Catholic, Muslim, Hindu, and Buddhist faiths.

Sadhu: Hindu holy man who renounces worldly possessions and seeks liberation from samsara.

Samsara: Cycle of life, from which the fortunate escape by living a blameless life full of contemplation into heaven or bliss.

Sangha: Community of Buddhist monks or bhikkhus, one of the "Three Jewels" of Buddhism, alongside the Buddha and the Dharma.

Semite: Originally applied to the descendants of Shem, eldest son of Noah, it is now applied to Jews, Phoenicians, Arabs, and Assyrians.

Sect: A branch of a faith with members who probably hold views quite different to the majority.

Shrine: Casket, altar, or chapel which honors a saint or god.

Stupas: Buddhist cairn containing a relic, forerunner to the pagoda.

Sura: Chapter of the Qur'an.

Tapu: Sacred and therefore prohibited, according to tribal belief. The root of the word *taboo*.

Theology: Study of religion and analysis of the nature of God and how it interacts with man.

Tirthankara: A great teacher of Jain philosophy and practice. Only two, Parsva and Mahavira, out of 24 are known to have lived.

Titans: In Greek mythology, a gigantic race whose kingdom preceded that of the gods.

Torah: First five books of the Old Testament, considered sacred by Jews.

Totemism: Belief found among tribespeople that they are descended from a particular animal or plant which is considered a guardian spirit.

Transcendental Meditation: Regular contemplation with the aid of a tailor-made mantra, it is a system strongly influenced by Hinduism and shot to fame when the Beatles became convinced of its benefits in 1967.

Transubstantiation: Catholic belief that by consecration the bread and wine of the Mass celebration becomes in nature the body and blood of Christ.

Upanishads: Hindu scriptures discussing human awareness and Brahman, the one reality.

Vaishnavism: Worship of the Hindu god Vishnu, the god who preserves and maintains life.

Vedas: Ancient Hindu scriptures.

Zionism: Movement founded in 1897 formed to promote Judaism and the reestablishment of a Jewish homeland.

INDEX

Pages in italics refer to illustrations